# Sharing Books Together:

*Promoting Emergent Literacy Through Reading Aloud and Home-School Partnerships*

**Kathleen A. Martin and L. Kay Emfinger**
University of Alabama at Birmingham

Photographs copyright © 2007, courtesy of the authors.
**Editor:** Subjects & Predicates Inc.

Published by
Southern Early Childhood Association
P.O. Box 55930
Little Rock, AR 72215-5930
www.SouthernEarlyChildhood.org
501-221-1648

**Sharing Books Together:**
*Promoting Emergent Literacy*
*Through Reading Aloud and*
*Home-School Partnerships*

Copyright © 2008 by the Southern Early Childhood Association.
ISBN #978-0942388-33-6

The contents of this book were developed under a grant from the United States Department of Education. However, the content does not necessarily represent the policy of the U.S. Department of Education, and it is not endorsed by the federal government.

## Preface

This book is designed for early childhood teachers and program directors. It has three chapters and extensive appendices.

**Chapter One** outlines important early literacy concepts that children can gain from listening to both fiction and nonfiction books being read aloud.

**Chapter Two** describes how early childhood teachers can develop effective home-school-community reading partnerships. The roles of home and community are described, with the focus on teachers of children ages 3 to 6. This chapter describes how to set up and administer classroom lending libraries and home-school literacy-related activities.

**Chapter Three** is an annotated bibliography of children's books available in inexpensive paperback format. While some fiction and classic children's literature titles are listed, nonfiction concept books are featured. Nonfiction books often are given less attention in early childhood classrooms, although they are equally effective in exploring early literacy concepts with emerging readers. Hands-on activities that promote a variety of essential early literacy concepts are included for each book.

**The Appendices** include forms and resource lists to help teachers and volunteers set up classroom libraries and home-school literacy programs.

Reading to and with children is a fascinating, rewarding endeavor for children, families, and teachers. We anticipate that this book will encourage a variety of early literacy activities at home, in family child care, and in group care settings.

**Kathleen A. Martin and L. Kay Emfinger**
*University of Alabama at Birmingham*
*October 2007*

# Contents

**Chapter 1 – The Values of Reading Aloud With Children** .........................6
   Why Read With Children? .........................7
   Oral Language Promotes Learning to Read .........................7
   Learning by Listening to Fiction .........................10
   Listening to Nonfiction Builds on Basic Concepts. .........................11
   Hearing Books and Stories: Early Reading Comprehension .........................13
   Reading Aloud Expands Vocabulary .........................14
   Sharing Books Contributes to Learning How Print Works .........................16
   Reading Aloud Promotes Phonological Awareness .........................17
   Reading Aloud Promotes Learning About Letters .........................20

**Chapter 2 – Community-Home-School Reading Partnerships** .........................22
   Community-Home-School Reading Partnerships .........................23
   What Can Communities Do? .........................23
   What Can Families Do? .........................25
   What Can Teachers Do? .........................25

**Chapter 3 – Children's Books and Related Early Literacy Activities** .........................37
   Curriculum Topics With Related Book Title .........................38
   Recommended Books and Learning Experiences .........................40

Appendices .........................82

**Appendix A**
Additional Readings .........................82

**Appendix B**
Resources for Educating the Community, Families, and Teachers .........................82

**Appendix C**
Resources to Organize a Lending Library .........................84
Sample Proposal for Funding .........................84
Children's Books .........................85
Checkout System Resources .........................85
Suppliers of Take-Home Literacy Packs .........................85
Teacher-Created Literacy Bag Resources .........................86
Take-Home Bag Vendors .........................86
Book Awards .........................86
Sources of Book-Related Items .........................86
Sample Library Procedures for Training Teachers and Volunteers .........................87

**Appendix D**
Resources for Involving Families .........................89
Sample Family Survey .........................89
Sample Family Orientation Flyer .........................89
Sample Family Orientation Agenda .........................89
Sample Family Orientation Handout .........................89
Sample Take-Home Tips .........................89
Sample Reading Log .........................90
Sample Reminder to Return Books .........................90

**References** .........................91

*When teachers select well-written books and books of interest to young children, explain new concepts and vocabulary, and share their pleasure in the books, the delight of learning to read is well on its way!*

# The Values of Reading Aloud With Children — Chapter 1

## Why Read With Children?

Reading interesting books with young children has two important benefits. The experience of sharing stories and their illustrations

- improves children's later literacy development (Anderson, Hiebert, Scott, & Wilkinson, 1985),
- increases children's motivation to learn to read (Greaney & Hegarty, 1987; Morrow & Young, 1997),
- helps children develop vocabulary knowledge (De Temple & Snow, 2003),
- introduces children to important concepts about how print works (Justice & Ezell, 2000; Justice & Ezell, 2002), and
- influences later reading comprehension abilities (Sayeski, Burgess, Pianta, & Lloyd, 2001).

Hearing high-quality picture books read by adults or older children gives younger children access to vocabulary and forms of language that may not be used in their everyday conversation. Reading to children promotes their awareness of how stories and printed materials work. In addition, reading to children helps them extend their knowledge of the world of ideas and concepts about it (Blok, 1999).

All these benefits contribute to success in learning to read, which is why reading to children in their early years is particularly important. The years from birth to age 6 are a critical period for learning language, both spoken and written. Many children spend as long as 10 hours a day in group care settings, often leaving families with limited time for reading and engaging in conversations about good books.

Additionally, children living in low-income families can especially benefit from an emphasis on reading at school, because they may live in communities with limited public access to books (Krashen, 1993), and their families may have fewer resources for providing books and magazines at home.

This chapter discusses understandings about oral and written language that teachers can explore with children from ages 3 to 6 while reading good picture books with them. Books often present many opportunities for children, families, and teachers to learn.

One of the most important reasons to read with children is the pleasure reading aloud brings to both readers and listeners. When children have early experiences with books they enjoy, it is a powerful incentive for them to want to learn to read (Sonnenschein & Munsterman, 2002). The shared experience of good books binds families, teachers, and children into a community of learners.

## Oral Language Promotes Learning to Read

Reading and writing are both based on a foundation of understanding language (Neuman & Dickinson, 2001; Snow, Burns, & Griffin, 1998). The two skills are expansions of abilities that children naturally develop from birth. Reading is related to listening, and writing is related to speaking.

---

*"Books to the ceiling,*

*Books to the sky,*

*My pile of books are [sic] a mile high.*

*How I love them!*

*How I need them!*

*I'll have a long beard by the time I read them."*

– Arnold Lobel

**Good books bind families, teachers, and children into a community of learners.**

*"Language is the dress of thought."*

– Samuel Johnson

## The Values of Reading Aloud With Children

- When listening and reading, people interact with another person's ideas in order to receive a message and make it their own (i.e., receptive language).

- When speaking and writing, people hope to engage other people and communicate to them their ideas, needs, or feelings (i.e. productive or expressive language).

All four processes (listening, speaking, reading, and writing) are forms of communication and are rooted in infancy. When babies cry, smile, coo, and move to gain their mother's or another caregiver's attention, communication is taking place in its earliest form. When the important adults in babies' lives respond to these attempts to impart messages, they support children's learning as well as their social/emotional development.

*Books present many opportunities for both children and teachers to learn.*

*One of the most important reasons to read with children is the pleasure reading aloud brings to both readers and listeners. The experience is a powerful incentive for children to want to learn to read.*

Children learn to talk through similar interactions. Babies and toddlers verbalize with many different sounds. Significant adults, who are likely to know what children want to communicate, respond appropriately and often expand the verbalization. For example, a toddler may reach toward animal crackers saying, "gee gee." When the adult responsively offers the child an animal cracker, the primary purpose of the child's communication has been accomplished, and the child comes to trust the adult to understand her or his needs.

If adults accompany their interactions with words such as "animal cracker" or a simple sentence, "Oh, you want an animal cracker," the communication is enriched – and presents children with natural opportunities to learn far more about language. Responses such as these have a major influence on children's language development (Heath, 1983).

Young children constantly experiment with language. When they receive support and feedback from adults and older children for their efforts, they learn how to communicate even more effectively. They learn new words and more complex ways of expressing what they mean. A child's oral language development is strongly related to later reading achievement (Catts, Fey, Zhang, & Tomblin, 1999; Scarborough, 1998; Storch & Whitehurst, 2002).

At the same time that preschool children are continuing to learn to communicate verbally, they also benefit from exploring language and symbols in printed form. They may recognize their favorite cereal box on the grocery store shelf, or they may come to understand that the red octagonal street sign means "STOP." Learning about language in printed forms (reading and writing) takes place at the same time that children are learning more about oral language (listening and speaking).

**Knowing about oral language supports exploration of printed language.**

Knowing about oral language strongly supports a child's exploration of printed language. The opposite also is true. Children learn many things about and through printed language that they can use in their spoken language.

**The opposite also is true.**

Although the two forms of language support one another, they are not the same. Spoken language is much more the language of "the here and now." Spoken language often has simpler forms and a more limited vocabulary than written language.

8

*Chapter 1*

**Young children constantly experiment with language.**

For example, in everyday speech people seldom use expressions such as, "Once upon a time" or "Over yonder hill." The vocabulary used in everyday speech also is simpler. In daily conversation people might say that a friend "was always getting mad at his brother." In a book, the same idea may be expressed as a friend who is "incessantly angry at his sibling." Children who are successful at learning to read have both the everyday language and the language of books as part of their literacy experience.

Language has many different purposes: to express feelings, to give directions, to inform, to find answers to questions, and to describe experiences, to name just a few. The purposes of any communication influence the structure of the language as well as the vocabulary. For example, poetry and other literary forms that often are used to express feelings often include special figures of speech such as simile and metaphor.

Eloise Greenfield's (2004) poem, "In the Land of Words" is a good illustration:

*In the land
of words,
I stand as still as a tree,
and let the words
rain down on me.*

"As still as a tree" is a simile. It paints a strong, clear image of how good literature communicates succinctly and with great power. "Words rain down" is a metaphor that compares the rush of beautiful words to falling raindrops. Neither expression is one that children are likely to hear in everyday speaking.

Books with practical purposes, that explain how to make something or how to perform a task, for example, are usually organized in a particular way and may rely on specialized vocabulary. For example, a recipe typically starts with a list of ingredients, followed by instructions about how to combine them. Words such "next" and "finally" may appear. An informational book that describes people, places, or things often will use the words, "although", "however", or the expression, "on the other hand". Language that a child hears in everyday conversations may not include these elements, but they are common in printed materials.

The more familiarity children have with all the language forms, varieties of expression, and kinds of vocabulary that are found in books, the easier it is to learn to read. Remember coming across a word for the first time in print? Sometimes it calls for a second look. "Oh, that's Albuquerque! So that's how it looks in print!" Beginning readers have that same kind of experience all the time. Any word in print has far more meaning – and is thus more memorable – when the word is familiar as a spoken word and the concept is understood already.

How can early childhood teachers help children develop these understandings about language and the rich vocabulary they need to be successful readers? The solution is all around – Read good books aloud with children!

The authors of high-quality children's picture books use a variety of language structures and rich, expressive vocabulary not found in typical everyday speech. They deal with ideas, emotions, concepts, people, and places that extend children's experiences. When children hear many books read to them, they gain experience with the more elaborate language of print as they take the first steps in learning to read.

Later, when they come across that language in the materials they are learning to read, it is easier for them to figure out the words, to analyze what the author means, and to predict what may come next in the book. When teachers

- select well-written picture books,
- choose topics of interest to young children,
- explain new concepts and vocabulary, and
- share their pleasure in the books, the delight of learning to read is well on its way!

## Learning by Listening to Fiction

*"The story always old and always new."*

Robert Browning

All good stories share the same elements:

- characters
- setting
- plot
- a problem or problems to solve
- resolution of the problem
- a deeper message the author wants to share

These elements are present in simple stories such as "The Three Little Pigs" or "The Three Billy Goats Gruff." More complex stories, including the latest best-selling adult novel, share the same elements, although certainly with more complicated organization.

After children understand how the parts of a story work together, they easily can make predictions about what is likely to happen next in a story. When beginning readers know, generally, how a story is likely to progress, they can comprehend most of the meaning while they attempt to figure out unfamiliar words from the context of the tale and by looking at the illustrations.

Children learn how stories work by hearing many, many stories. Those who have much experience listening to books and oral tales have been introduced to all sorts of characters with a wide variety of challenges that need to be solved. These stories give children a sampling of the many possible ways to solve problems.

When adult readers talk with children about the deeper messages shared by authors, children soon take delight in finding those messages for themselves. Looking for the underlying message, sometimes called a moral, is the beginning of being able to make inferences, to read between the lines to construct meaning beyond the literal words. Having the ability to make inferences while reading is an important skill in developing higher levels of proficiency in reading. This skill can be very difficult for young readers who have not had opportunities to find the deeper meanings in stories they have heard.

## Listening to Nonfiction Builds on Basic Concepts

The world is filled with ideas, knowledge, information, and wonder. An important goal of high-quality early childhood programs is to expand children's awareness of that world. One of the best rewards of teaching these young ages is the opportunity to observe and explore children's curiosity (their need to know why and how) with them. Children's desire to know, and the questions they want answered, easily can go beyond information any teacher may know.

Nonfiction books bring the world of ideas to the classroom. Age-appropriate nonfiction books are available on almost any subject. Helping children develop basic concepts in content areas such as science, math, and social studies is fascinating in itself, and lays the foundation for more in-depth subject-area learning in elementary school and the rest of their lives.

Of course, concept development requires far more than just hearing words in books. Children must participate in active learning that includes handling real objects; exploring through free play; following through with pretend play, music, art, and movement; engaging in guided investigation, as well as conducting trial-and-error experiments. Children need to explore, interact, act, observe, and reflect on the process and consequences of their actions.

Sensitive and clever teachers incorporate picture books into every day's planned explorations. An informational book can become the introduction to hands-on activities that build deep understandings. For example, sharing a book about community helpers before a field trip to the police or fire station is an effective introduction to concepts that will develop further with first-hand experiences. Reviewing it afterward can give children opportunities to reflect on their experiences and become even more familiar with the meaning of the book.

Often fiction and nonfiction books on similar topics can be paired to explore a topic in different ways. For example, *Officer Buckle and Gloria* (Rathman, 1995) provides a different view of how police serve communities than does the nonfiction book, *Police Officers Protect People* (Greene, 1997). Children who listen to and talk about both books get a more complex view of police officers than do children who only discuss one of the books.

Concept knowledge is related to reading success and to the development of expanded vocabulary. When children already know something about the topic of a book, they use that prior knowledge to understand and interpret the new ideas in the book.

One significant reason that young readers may find a book hard to grasp is simply that they have no first-hand experience with the topic. Children from the city who have no knowledge of a farm or farm animals may find reading a book, even a very simple book, about the farm very baffling. Sheep and goats look confusingly similar. Chickens, geese, and ducks also are easily mixed up if someone has never encountered them.

Learning new words is easier when children already have some familiarity with the concept. For example, learning the meaning of "terrible" is much easier when children

*"The world is so full of a number of things, I'm sure we should all be as happy as kings."*

Robert Louis Stevenson

already know something about things that seem bad or scary. Additionally, if children understand the oral concept of "terrible", they will more easily recognize the written word when it is introduced.

Sharing nonfiction texts can be challenging because informational books do not have the same structure as stories. While all stories share the same elements and a common basic structure, nonfiction books are organized in many different ways. An information book that describes the life cycle of butterflies will have features and an organization very different from a biography or a book that describes how to make a mask, for instance.

If children approach an informational book expecting to find characters, setting, and a plot, they will be puzzled. Beginning readers who have little experience listening to and talking about nonfiction books often experience great difficulty reading them independently and understanding what they have read. This lack of experience may result in a child's reading level for nonfiction being much lower than the reading level for stories (Leslie & Caldwell, 2005).

Teachers can help prevent these difficulties by sharing an assortment of both fiction and informational books with children, and by explaining the many ways these are organized. Thoughtful introductions to a nonfiction book can alert children to the features they will find while listening.

Children who have lots of experiences as listeners and analyzers of meaning have a desire to learn to read independently, and they appreciate the pleasure, excitement, and personal satisfaction that come from reading!

### How to Introduce Animal Books

For example, informational books about animals often describe the life cycle, explain what they eat, and describe where they live. When introducing *Monarch Butterfly* (Gibbons, 1991), a discussion such as the following alerts children as to what to expect and gives children concrete ideas to look for during the reading. Allow time for children to contribute to the discussion, even recording their comments as a guide for future follow-up experiences.

> The title of this book is *Monarch Butterfly*. What do you think the book is about?
>
> Yes, it's a book about butterflies. But it's not a pretend story. It's a book with all kinds of facts about Monarch butterflies. What would you like to know about Monarch butterflies?
>
> What else might be interesting to learn about Monarch butterflies? What do you think the book might say about caterpillars?
>
> What do you think the author may tell us about what caterpillars eat? Where they live?
>
> Let's find out!

### Ways to Introduce Books With Directions

An introduction to a book that gives directions needs to be tailored in another way because the structure of these books is different. When building interest in a book like

*How to Make Salsa* (Lucerno, 1966), readers alert listeners that the text is organized in a specific way.

> Who has ever helped someone cook?
>
> Before you started, what did you do? Oh, you helped your dad fix pancakes!
>
> What ingredients go in pancakes? What did you put in the bowl first? What came next? Then what did you do?
>
> The name of this book is *How to Make Salsa*. Who has eaten salsa? What do you think we might find inside this book?
>
> What would you need to know if you wanted to make salsa?
>
> Let's read and see if we can learn how to make it.

When the introduction alerts listeners to the book's organization, children can anticipate what they are about to hear (or as beginning readers, what they are about to read), and they are much better able to attend to the information and to remember what they have heard or read. Discussion before reading a book provides a scaffold for the children to learn the concepts within its pages.

*Discussion before reading provides a scaffold for children to learn concepts.*

## Hearing Books and Stories: Early Reading Comprehension

When children come to elementary school with many experiences listening to books, they start with a huge advantage. Children who have been read to many times will have accumulated these types of learnings:

- already know that a book contains messages from the author
- know how to be flexible in the ways they listen to different kinds of books so they understand the author's message
- are familiar with written language found in books
- have developed many concepts beyond their personal experiences
- have learned many words that they are likely to find in other books that they will learn to read
- know that they will find experiences that reflect people and events in their lives
- expect to encounter information and ideas that expand their understandings
- know how to make logical predictions
- realize that important messages are often found "between the lines"
- make personal connections to the book content or theme
- know how to handle and care for books

*"'Tis the good reader that makes the good book."*

– Ralph Waldo Emerson

## The Values of Reading Aloud With Children

- link the author's ideas to things they understand already
- realize how words and illustrations work together to communicate
- are comfortable reflecting on the meaning of books with others
- are eager to explore books more

Children who have lots of experiences as listeners and analyzers of meaning have a desire to learn to read independently, and they appreciate the pleasure, excitement, and personal satisfaction that come from reading!

## Reading Aloud Expands Vocabulary

*"What do you read, my lord? Words, words, words."*

– Shakespeare (Hamlet)

What is vocabulary? Why is expanding children's vocabularies so important? How can teachers of young children teach vocabulary effectively? Vocabulary is simply all the words a person knows.

People know different words for different aspects of communication. The sets of words people understand are different when they

- listen (listening vocabulary),
- talk (speaking vocabulary),
- write (writing vocabulary), or
- recognize when reading (reading vocabulary).

The sets of vocabulary words overlap, but many words are not likely to be in every set. Having a word in one set makes it easier to add that word to another set. Children who understand many spoken words will be able to add those words to spoken vocabulary and will find those words easier to read.

High-quality children's picture books are filled with descriptive words, words that express feelings, and words that represent important concepts about how the world works. Many of these words are words children will never hear in typical everyday conversations. Reading books aloud gives the teacher or other reader a built-in opportunity to help children develop a large listening vocabulary that can more readily become reading vocabulary when formal instruction begins.

All children build vocabulary when adults or older siblings share books with them. Teachers of children with few reading opportunities at home – and children who are learning English as a second language – have a particular responsibility to incorporate vocabulary learning as a goal for their language development.

All families support their children's language learning, and all families want their children to succeed in school as well as life. The support for realizing these dreams, however, varies according to the resources and circumstances of each family. Sometimes the families' style of support is different from the expectations at school (Heath, 1983; McDonald Connor, Son, Hindman, & Morrison, 2005; Reese, Cox, Harte, & McAnally, 2003). With respectful guidance, families at all economic levels and speaking any home language can provide strong support for English vocabulary and language development (Mass & Cohen, 2006; Taylor & Dorsey-Gaines, 1988).

Research studies consistently indicate that

- children's vocabulary is related to success in reading and reading comprehension in elementary school (Goswami, 2001; Muter, Hulme, & Snowling, 2004; Rupley, 2005)
- differences in vocabulary can be noted as early as 3 years of age (Hart & Risley, 1995)
- the preschool years are critical for learning vocabulary (Dickinson & Tabors, 2001)

Children from middle-class homes (Hart & Risley, 1995) where parents love to read themselves (Bus, 2001) and share books and writing with children (Sulzby & Edwards, 1993) have larger vocabularies. High-quality early childhood programs offer opportunities for all children to have these advantages because teachers make the best use of reading books and other language experiences in their classrooms.

Simply hearing a word will not make it part of a child's vocabulary, but by using a number of practical, proven strategies, teachers of young children can make the best use of the vocabulary opportunities books provide. These techniques are briefly described here.

**Preview the Book!**

Wise teachers always read a book before reading it to children, even if the book is familiar! Previewing the book enables teachers to think about what this group of children needs to know before the book can make sense to them.

Careful previewing makes it possible for a teacher to give an enthusiastic book introduction. Look for ways to relate the book to these children's experiences. Choose illustrations to highlight and discuss. Explain things that may be confusing. Offer concrete items related to the book for children to touch (corn cobs, fabric, eggs). Let children know what to expect from the book without giving away the resolution of the problem or the surprise at the end.

**Explain New Vocabulary Words**

An effective preview includes noticing words in the book that children may not understand. For example, "The name of this book is *Along Came Greedy Cat*. Who knows someone who is greedy? What does that word "greedy" mean?"

Make best use of the opportunity to teach vocabulary by pausing while reading the story to give an additional explanation when an unfamiliar word is used. For example: "He was eating everything Mom put in the shopping bag. My goodness! He was greedy!" The most effective teachers then follow the reading with questions that use the new words. For example, "How do you know this is a greedy cat?" The context in which the

**Always read a book before reading it to children!**

# The Values of Reading Aloud With Children

word is used, and the nearby illustrations, are often helpful for children to figure out what a word means.

### Use New Words in Context

Teachers continue to use the new words during the day and throughout the week by working them into conversations with children. "Anthony is sharing his crackers with Tiffany. Would we say that Anthony is being greedy or generous?"

When children hear a new word, link it to another word or to a concept they understand. Plan several opportunities for children to hear and use it, so it can become part of their listening or speaking vocabularies. To follow up with the word "greedy", children might engage in a community service project to show their generosity and caring for others. Teaching and learning about words every day makes the classroom an exciting, lively place in which to learn and practice positive behaviors.

## Sharing Books Contributes to Learning How Print Works

When children begin formal instruction in reading, they are likely to be given directions such as, "Look at the first word on the page" or "Find the first letter of the word." While such statements seem simple, following them requires complex understandings. What is a letter? What is a word? How are letters and words related? How do I know which is the first letter or the first word? In which direction do I look?

Clay (2005) described 20 different print concepts that children acquire by the time they are 7 years old. The list here identifies 11 of Clay's concepts that most children have developed before they are 6 years old.

**Work new words into conversations with children.**

*"He who first shortened the labour of copyists by device of Movable Types was… creating a whole new democratic world."*

– Thomas Carlyle

> **Important Concepts About English Print That Children Develop Before Age 6**
> - Where is the front of the book?
> - The print, rather than the picture, usually contains the key message.
> - When reading, there is a corresponding written word for every word that is spoken (one-to-one voice/print match).
> - The first word on a page is the one on the top line that is closest to the left edge.
> - Readers direct attention left to right across the line of print.
> - Which way do I go when I get to the end of the line? (return sweep)
> - What is meant by "first" and "last" parts of sentence, paragraph, page, and whole story?
> - How do I orient myself to the pictures? (know when a picture is upside down)
> - How do I orient myself to the print? (know when print is upside down)
>   Note: Knowing if the print is upside down is important to learn many letters such as u, n, b, p).
> - When two facing pages have print, which one do I read first?
> - A word is a group of letters clustered together with space on either side.
>
> Adapted from *An Observation Survey of Early Literacy Achievement* by M.M. Clay (2005).

Understanding these print concepts is related to success in beginning reading (Chaney, 1998; Levy, Gong, Hessels, Evans, & Jared, 2005; Scarborough, 1998). These concepts represent the background understandings essential to making sense of more formal reading instruction. Many children who have been exposed to books throughout their preschool years develop these understandings without any direct teaching. Teachers can include discussion of print concepts naturally in the course of sharing books with individual children or with the whole class. Children in elementary school who have not had many experiences with books need someone to explain and demonstrate these important ideas.

Many times teachers share regular-sized books with the class, with small groups, or even individual children. When the purpose of the sharing is to hear and respond to a good story, actually seeing the print is not always necessary, if the pictures are visible to everyone. However, when the teacher plans to explain print concepts, children must actually see the print, not just the pictures.

When sharing books with small groups and with individual children during center time, a teacher using a regular-sized book can be effective. When discussing print concepts with a larger group, however, large-format (big) books ensure all children can see the details of the print. These are a few strategies commonly used with big books.

- One effective strategy for talking about print concepts is to "think out loud" about some of the decisions a reader must make. For example, a teacher using a finger or a pointer while reading a large-format book to a group can come to the end of a line of print, stop, and say, "M-m-m-m, I've run out of print to read. Who can tell me where I need to look to find the next word?"

- A teacher can demonstrate the concept of word by covering important words with highlighter tape. This tape is easy to remove without damaging pages. For example, after reading a rhyming book to the class several times, the transparent tape can mark the two rhyming words at the ends of consecutive lines. Children will be thrilled to respond when asked to point to "the word that says Jill" and "the word that says hill."

- Teachers can demonstrate the concept of letter by asking children to find (on any page, as well as signs, boxes, and other print sources) the letters that begin their names. Using a pointer (with a large-format book) or a finger (with other items), point to the words one-to-one while reading. This helps children understand the voice/print match.

These techniques bring added learning dimensions to story reading and prepare children for success as beginning readers.

## Reading Aloud Promotes Phonological Awareness

English is an alphabetic language, meaning that written English uses alphabet letters to represent sounds of speech. One important aspect of learning to read is learning how the

*Learning about language in printed forms (reading and writing) takes place at the same time that children are learning more about oral language (listening and speaking). Spoken language is much more the language of "the here and now." Spoken language often has simpler forms and a more limited vocabulary than written language.*

## The Values of Reading Aloud With Children

system of representation works. Mastering letter/sound relationships (phonics) requires the construction of sophisticated concepts about language sounds, as well as identifying each of the letters.

First, think about how spoken English works. It consists of many interrelated sounds that work together to express thoughts and feelings. When saying the sentence, "Joseph kicked the ball outside the fence," the whole spoken sentence can be thought of as a chunk of sound, but that chunk consists of smaller sounds working together.

When generally referring to the ability to hear all the different sounds in spoken language, linguists use the term phonological awareness. This term includes

- hearing words in sentences,
- hearing syllables in words,
- hearing the parts of a syllable, and
- hearing the individual sounds represented by letters.

### Individual Words

One early understanding about language sounds that children develop is the realization that spoken words can be heard individually within a stream of speech. For the example sentence about Joseph, a young child who knows Joseph is likely to hear the sentence and know exactly who was responsible for kicking the ball outside the fence. Young children also probably have the experience to know what it means to kick, what balls and fences are, and where outside the fence would be located.

Children's names are often the first individual words they recognize, in speaking and in print. Refer to their names often – such as the nametags on their cubbies – to indicate that each name is separate. To help children recognize individual words in print, teachers can point to words one-to-one when reading. Point out words found on signs (exit, STOP), food containers, T-shirts, and other everyday places. Another strategy to help children recognize words and syllables is to ask them to clap the words while reading a sentence aloud.

### Syllables

**Syllables are bursts of sound!**

As young children become more aware of words, they discover that some words are longer and work differently from others (Kamii & Manning, 1999). A word such as "hat" has a single burst of sound; however, "because" has two sound bursts. The technical term for these bursts of sound within a word is "syllable". Words have as many syllables as they have vowel sounds.

Young children often enjoy saying and clapping the syllables of long, multisyllable words (all-i-ga-tor; beau-ti-ful, ter-ri-ble) that are found in stories. Well-written children's books are filled with examples teachers can use to help children develop this understanding. Hearing syllables contributes to later success in reading long, multisyllable words in print.

# Chapter 1

## Onsets and Rimes

Although most people don't usually think about it, syllables have parts, also.

- The word "window" has two syllables (win-dow).
- Each syllable also has two parts, (w-in) and (d-ow).
- The consonant part of the syllable is the onset (w, d).
- The rest of the syllable is the rime (-in, -ow).

The rime starts with the vowel in the syllable and includes the vowel and the letters that follow the vowel. It is the rime in the syllable that makes words rhyme. Understanding how onset and rime work helps beginning readers figure out many words. For example, a child who can read the word "can", and who understands onset and rime, can read "fan", "man", and "plan", as well.

Learning the definitions of onset and rime is not appropriate or necessary for young children. However, teachers can help children develop the knowledge they need about onset and rime by drawing attention to words that rhyme. They help children hear how the words sound alike by asking children to repeat them.

For example, a teacher might say "Jack and JILL went up the HILL. M-m-m-m-m I heard two words that sound alike, did you?" "Let's say those two words, Jill, hill. Do you hear it? They end the same. They rhyme. Let's listen to the rest of the poem and see if we can find any more words that rhyme."

When teachers also show children how many English rhyming words look alike at the ends, even deeper learning occurs. Teachers can show children word families (cat, sat, fat, mat, splat) that can be charted for a classroom word wall. Books of nursery rhymes, songs, poems, and chants offer many natural opportunities for these explorations of both sound and print similarities.

## Phonemes

The smallest unit of spoken sound is called a phoneme. Phonemes are represented by letters, but are not the same things as letters. A phoneme is what one hears; a letter is what one sees. When linguists talk about children being able to hear these smallest speech sounds, they use the term phonemic awareness.

A child having phonemic awareness understands that the word "sat" can be thought of as having three sounds: /s/, /a/, and /t/. When one says the word out loud slowly and tries not to think of the letters, just the sounds – those are the phonemes.

If one says the word "boat" the same way, it, too, has three phonemes, /b/, /o/, and /t/, but it has four letters. Being able to hear phonemes within words and syllables is the last step that develops in the complex understanding about the sounds of any language (Goswami & Bryant, 1990). Beginning readers use these understandings of sounds and sound sequences as they look at the sequences of letters in words they are trying to read (Goswami & Bryant, 1990; Whitehurst & Lonigan, 2001).

---

*When adult readers talk with children about the deeper messages shared by authors, children soon take delight in finding those messages for themselves. Looking for the underlying message is the beginning of being able to read between the lines to construct meaning beyond the literal words. Having the ability to make inferences while reading is an important skill in developing higher levels of proficiency in reading.*

# The Values of Reading Aloud With Children

Adults help children develop phonemic awareness when they share books that feature rhyme and alliteration. Alliteration is the repetition of the same speech sound in several words in a series. The title of the book *Four Famished Foxes and Fosdyke* (Duncan, 1997) is an example. Tongue twisters such as "Peter Piper," and "She Sells Sea Shells" are fun to learn and also contribute to understanding language sounds.

Many researchers and language development experts agree that the best way to develop all the different types of phonological awareness is through experiences with books, songs, and rhymes (Bear, Ivernizzi, Templeton, & Johnston, 2000; Cunningham, 1990; Snow, Burns, & Griffin, 1998; Yopp, 1995). Stories, tongue twisters, poems, songs, and nursery rhymes are much more fun – and far more appealing and memorable – than isolated skill activities such as flashcards or drills. Learning through activities with books has the added benefit of demonstrating for children how language sounds are related to reading.

## Reading Aloud Promotes Learning About Letters

Letter knowledge is a strong predictor of future success in learning to read (Bishop, 2003; Jansky & de Hirsch, 1972; Muter, Hulme, & Snowling, 2004; Ritchey & Speece, 2006; Scanlon & Vellutino, 1996; Scarborough, 2001). Letter knowledge, while it seems simple on the surface, actually involves several more complicated concepts. It is much more than just singing the "Alphabet Song."

*Adults help children develop phonemic awareness when they share books that feature rhyme and alliteration. Alliteration is the repetition of the same speech sound in several words in a series.*

Letter knowledge includes:

- grasping the concept of how letters are grouped together in a specific sequence to make a word

- knowing the name of a particularly detailed shape that is not exactly the same each time. For example a, *a*, **a**, and **a** are all the same letter, as are A, *A*, *A*, and **A**. Even in books that beginners read, the same letter will not look the same in every book.

- identifying the ways that letters are used to represent speech sounds. When children learn the names of the letters, they begin a long process of learning the complex letter/sound relationships in English. Saying the names of most letters produces one of the sounds that the letter represents. For example, when verbalizing the name of the letter A, the long vowel sound that letter represents is spoken. When saying the name of the letter T, the first part of the verbalization is the speech sound the letter represents.

Classrooms for young children typically provide many opportunities to learn letters and their names. Alphabet charts, magnetic letters, alphabet blocks, and other alphabet

# Chapter 1

manipulatives such as rubber stamps and sandpaper letters give children many ways to experience letters. When teachers model writing for children and encourage children to write, children begin to learn how letters are related to writing words. When letter learning is included as part of book sharing, children begin to understand the role of letters in reading. Writing with children and incorporating letter learning as part of book sharing both provide meaningful contexts for learning letters.

**Letter knowledge is much more than just singing the "Alphabet Song."**

Of course, sharing alphabet books with children is a logical and important way to use books to help children learn letters. Alphabet books are wonderful tools for developing the understanding that the same letter can look a little different each time. While alphabet books certainly help children learn about letters, any book shared with children presents occasions for letter learning.

Children often begin letter learning with the letters in their names. After all, for a young child, these are very important and familiar letters. After reading a big book, a teacher can give several children a piece of highlighter tape and ask them to find a letter. A teacher may ask the child to find the first letter in his name. For example, "Carlos, can you come up and find a c on this page? C is the first letter in your name." Or, several children may be asked to find the same letter: "This page has a lot of As. Can you come up and find one, Tiffany?"

Sometimes children learn to recognize simple, important words such as "No," "Yes," "Stop" or their own names. Often these words are recognized as a whole without the child actually knowing the names of the letters or even without knowing that the word is made of letters.

When children know words (including names) in this way, teachers can enrich the learning by pointing out how letters go together to make the word. For example, after sharing the big book *Along Came Greedy Cat* (Cowley, 1983) many times with the class while using a pointer, some children will be able to find the word cat. By using a small card or hands to cover parts of the word, a teacher can show children how that word has three letters: c, a, and t. The teacher might say, "Those three letters go together and make the word cat."

Learning that occurs during the early years is the foundation for future school success, particularly in reading. There are so many literacy concepts that children need to know when they start school! It is comforting to remember that the single most important thing adults can do to ensure that children become successful readers is to read books with them.

Reading high-quality picture books; talking about stories and concepts; thinking out loud about how readers make decisions; and pointing out features of books, words, and letters all contribute to future literacy success. The book titles and activities found in Chapter Three of this volume provide many examples of using books to help children gain important literacy concepts. The authors anticipate that after trying just a few of the ideas, teachers and families will enjoy inventing their own hands-on ideas for extending the reading of these and many other books with children.

*Take-home book packets and activities from a classroom lending library can provide parents with a convenient, powerful way to support their children's literacy development every day.*

# Community-Home-School Reading Partnerships

Teachers alone cannot achieve the tremendous challenge to produce a "nation of readers" (Anderson, Hiebert, Scott, & Wilkinson, 1985). Homes, schools, and communities must forge partnerships to promote literacy. People must come together to encourage children and show them the way along the delightful path of reading.

Although it has long been widely accepted that reading aloud is the single most important act for promoting reading success (Anderson, Hiebert, Scott, & Wilkinson, 1985), children come to school with a wide variety of book experiences. A child who is read to for just 20 minutes every day beginning at birth arrives in kindergarten with 600 hours of shared literacy experiences, while others have few, if any, hours becoming familiar with books in the company of a loving adult.

The time adults spend reading storybooks to children has long been correlated with the level of child's oral language development (Barrentine, 1996; Durkin, 1966). In addition to book *experiences*, book *access* influences children's literacy development. Children who have books readily accessible in the home, learn to read earlier (Appleby, Langer, & Mullis, 1988).

This chapter provides a blueprint for action at the community, family, and classroom levels to narrow the gap of high-quality children's picture book access and experience. Because the audience of this book is primarily teachers, classroom-level action will be detailed while other facets are briefly described.

## What Can Communities Do?

"It takes a village to raise a child." – Ancient African Proverb

This old adage is especially true when applied to the area of children's literacy. Public awareness, access to resources and services, and educational support are the three pillars of community activism on behalf of children's learning.

### Increase Public Awareness

Community organizations, such as the United Way program *Success By Six*, literacy councils, local schools, and libraries often collaborate to develop media campaigns to promote community awareness of literacy benchmarks and of the importance of reading aloud as a tool to increase early literacy learning.

The goals of public television's *Between the Lions® Designated Reader* campaign are to raise awareness and ensure that every child is read aloud to daily. The program also provides support and information for companies and community centers wishing to organize storybook sessions in child care centers, libraries, and schools, or to arrange for children to come on the work site for the experience.

Awareness about the importance of early literacy improves community commitment to provide these experiences for young children and support funding for quality book access and experiences.

---

*"Few children learn to read books by themselves. Someone has to lure them into the wonderful world of the written word; someone has to show them the way."*

– Orville Prescott
(1965, in Trelease, 2001, p. 60)

**Book *experiences* and *access* influence literacy development.**

**Promote community awareness.**

## Community-Home-School Reading Partnerships

### Improve Access to Resources

Access to services and resources within a community often requires funding and soliciting support from key leaders to provide the necessary infrastructure. Cooperation among agencies and programs to eliminate duplication and serve unfilled niches is also a successful strategy. Access to books is multifaceted, and may include libraries, classrooms, and organizations providing books to keep in the home. Many of these services are described in more detail, with contact information, in Appendix B.

**Increase library access.** Community leaders can survey all areas to ensure that library locations are accessible to people who rely on public transportation or must walk. Libraries can be urged to extend hours and programming (story times, author visits, dial-a-story) to meet the needs of working families. With tight budgets, additional volunteers may be needed to accomplish these important goals for supporting early literacy.

**Make browsing convenient.** Community book projects such as *Literacy, Inc. (LINC)* provide children's book browsing baskets in places that families frequent most – fast-food restaurants, churches, beauty shops, and auto repair shops, for example.

*Teachers of young children can provide support, encouragement, information, and resources to enable families to increase literacy activities with their children at home.*

**Add to home collections.** Book give-away projects (such as *Reach Out and Read, Reading Is Fundamental, KEEP Books,* and *First Books*) that target low-income families can be coordinated to provide sustainable ongoing services.

**Expand classroom libraries.** The *Children's Literacy Initiative* is an example of mobilizing community resources to establish libraries in the places where young children spend most of their time, family child care homes and centers. Five to eight books per child is the minimum number that most experts recommend. However, many early care settings fall short of this benchmark (Neuman, Celano, Greco, & Shue, 2001).

*Early Reading First*, a federally funded initiative, provides much needed resources to the early education community, along with a comprehensive accountability component that involves training and assessment. Explore local funding sources as well.

**Expand other initiatives.** Community-based support services providing story-reading experiences for at-risk children vary from locally developed programs to networks of projects such as *Jumpstart,* an AmeriCorps program. Jumpstart is a tutoring model that enables college-student AmeriCorps members to develop meaningful one-on-one relationships with 3- to 5- year olds as they volunteer from 300 to 525 hours per school year. AmeriCorps members are awarded educational stipends that can be used to pay for their education in return for their service to preschoolers.

### Support Early Education

There are two main veins of educational support and training that communities can offer:

- programs targeting teachers and caregivers of young children, and
- programs for families

24

Teacher education and parenting resources are also described in Appendix B.

Teacher training includes formalized regional efforts (i.e., *Children's Literacy Initiative*), state and national efforts (*Heads Up! Network*), and local efforts (local child care resource and referral agencies).

Parent supports range from those developed by local literacy councils, schools, and libraries to packaged curricula such as *Motheread*, *Even Start Family Literacy*, and *Parents as Teachers*.

## What Can Families Do?

"Considerable research suggests that skeptics [of parent involvement] are probably mistaken... Schools and families can work together to help children succeed academically. This proposition is especially true for early literacy." – Goldenberg (2002, p. 221)

Parents, grandparents, and older siblings are children's first and most powerful teachers (Talan, 1990). Families can support early literacy by purchasing children's books for reading at home or by borrowing books from a library. However, having books in the home is only one side of the reading coin. Other key factors include a supportive adult (Morrow, 1983) and routine storybook reading (Bus, van Ijzendoorn, & Pellegrini, 1995).

A supportive adult is a person involved in the child's daily life who engages in story reading with the child on a regular basis. Supportive adults can be family members, neighbors, and friends. Nearly all families and caregivers are interested in supporting their children's literacy development, but some may need encouragement and recommendations about the most effective ways to promote early reading skills. Teachers of young children can provide support, encouragement, information, and resources to enable families to increase literacy activities with their children at home.

Families also can play a major role in establishing home-school partnerships, offering ideas for services, volunteering in various capacities, and giving feedback about the usefulness of the initiatives. Collaborative partnerships among families and teachers is essential for the success of any early literacy effort.

## What Can Teachers Do?

"Kids not only need to read a lot but they need lots of books they can read right at their fingertips. They also need access to books that entice them, attract them to reading. Schools... can make it easy and unrisky for children to take books home for the evening or weekend by worrying less about losing books to children and more about losing children to illiteracy." – Richard L. Allington (2000, p. 68)

First, teachers and parents must collaborate as partners. Home visits, parent workshops, phone calls, notes, and newsletters are primary vehicles for sharing explicit information about literacy development and the importance of reading aloud to children (Brown, 1994; Vukelich, Christie, & Enz, 2002).

While teachers can inform families about how they can help support classroom literacy learning, that strategy is only the beginning of the partnership. *Two-way communication* is the key to forging successful partnerships with children's families. When teachers provide multiple ways for families to be heard and become involved in early literacy efforts, better communications result. Families who have a variety of opportunities to interact with teachers in ways that match their differing *skills and comfort levels* are more likely to feel respected and to participate.

Providing families with access to resources is the second cornerstone of a successful family literacy program. Classroom lending libraries and take-home activity packets are two effective ways to bridge the book gap (Brock & Dodd, 1994). For many parents who work long hours, the last stop of the evening is an after-care program to pick up their children – not the library. So little time... so much to do. Families prioritize their time to meet the bare essentials of dinner preparation and supervision of bath time and bedtime routines. Take-home book packets and activities from a classroom lending library can provide parents with a convenient, powerful way to support their children's literacy development every day.

### How does a program start a classroom lending library?

A classroom lending library provides ready access to new worlds – both real and imaginary. This access is only one of the joyful "somethings" take-home books provide for families. The goals of a classroom lending library program are to:

- Provide families with more and accurate information on literacy development so that parents and teachers have the same goals and expectations for young children;

- Provide famiies with guidance on how to share books with their children; and to

- Provide families with books and materials to increase their children's literacy skills.

Suggestions for the overall design and arrangement of the classroom library, including guidelines for creating cozy, inviting spaces, have been detailed in other publications (Morrow & Weinstein, 1986; Morrow, 2001, batTzedek, 2002) and are not included here. Only resources related specifically to the parent-child lending library are detailed.

The first decision to be made is whether to have the parent/child take-home library and the classroom library as one-and-the-same or separate entities. Both options have pros and cons. Having a limited number of books for children to take home enables teachers to build a separate library of inexpensive books. Thus, any book losses are not as costly.

However, schools choosing to have classroom book collections separate from the parent/child take-home lending library risk having classroom learning experiences that are disjointed from home activities. Children who can access the entire classroom library have the opportunity to select favorites from read-aloud sessions to share with family members, which provides continuity in learning. Whether there are two separate libraries or one, the guidelines for contents and organization are the same.

*"I like a teacher who gives you something to take home to think about besides homework."*

–Lily Tomlin as Edith Ann

# Chapter 2

**What types of books should be included in a lending library?**

The classroom library should reflect the holdings of a good public library's children's section, including these categories:

- picture books
- traditional literature from a variety of cultures (folktales, fables, fairy tales, nursery rhymes)
- concept books (such as alphabet, counting, colors, shapes)
- songs, poems, and rhyming books
- wordless books
- favorite characters stories (*Curious George, Madeline, Clifford*)
- non-fiction books that support classroom learning experiences (plants, animals, dinosaurs, cultures, communities, social skills, holidays)
- easy-to-read-books

Widely respected and award-winning authors (see Appendix C) that represent high-quality literature should be the foundation of any classroom library (Bennett-Armistead, Duke, & Moses, 2005). Including some books that parents find readily accessible at dollar and grocery stores also is recommended as a way to support families with limited resources by affirming the value of these books as well. Teachers are urged to read all books before purchase to assure that the messages, vocabulary, and illustrations are suitable.

**How do programs get books for a classroom lending library?**

Paperback books are an affordable way to stock a classroom library. Book clubs for young children offer high-quality inexpensive paperback books (see Appendix C). Bonus points awarded with purchases can also be used to acquire more books, recordings, and hands-on book characters such as puppets.

Yard sales, thrift stores, donations from children's families (as part of a birthday celebration, perhaps), book drives held by business partners, classroom adoption by a higher grade level or another school, books made by students including those in upper grades, and books from local literacy councils are just a few of the many sources for books.

Most bookstores give teachers 15 to 20% discounts for classroom purchases. Local businesses, educational foundations, civic groups, and churches fund small grants for innovative classroom activities.

Book-lending libraries are often eligible for grants (see a sample funding proposal in Appendix C) because book checkout records provide the documentation often needed as part of the grant accountability. Resources provided by the funding are almost immediately catapulted back into the community in a most visible way. When books

---

*An inviting, attractive lending library will draw in children and their families. Easy access to an appealing, well-organized collection will keep them returning for more. Books should be attractively displayed so that covers face outward for easy viewing.*

**Read all books before purchase.**

**Recognize the funder with a label in the book.**

purchased with grant funds have an acknowledgement label in the front, the funder receives immediate and on-going recognition, and the funder becomes associated with the importance of reading aloud daily.

### What kinds of book displays are most appealing?

An inviting, attractive lending library will draw in children and their families. Easy access to an appealing, well-organized collection will keep them returning for more. Books should be attractively displayed so that covers face outward for easy viewing. Book displays can be in a variety of tiered, stationary, and stable revolving shelves. Bins or wheeled carts can hold duplicate copies.

**Shelves.** Traditional book shelves and tiered book displays come in affordable wire and plastic versions as well as more costly but far sturdier wood versions. Traditional shelves hold more books than tiered shelving. Some books might be placed in groups on the shelves in plastic or woven baskets or crates. All displays should be eye-level height for children. Be creative with book displays. Window boxes, gutters, cove molding, and narrow wire over-the-door pantry shelving are just a few ideas.

**Special displays.** At least two frequently changing displays should be featured at all times. Collections of books could be organized around a theme, genre, or authors/illustrators, and rotated every couple of weeks. For example, one display may contain books by Mem Fox (this technique is called an author study) while non-fiction books about Australia could be a theme-related display. Displays encourage children to take home books related to current classroom topics, thus providing an authentic vehicle for connecting home and school.

**Other attractions.** Along with books in the library area, consider displaying a variety of appealing, book-related items such as these (see also Appendix C):

- attractive posters about books and reading
- plush, stuffed book characters (Clifford, Franklin)
- puppets, action figures, and dolls
- storybook flannel boards and props
- displays about children's book authors and illustrators
- magnetic, felt, and sticky boards
- games, puzzles, and toys
- activity books
- CDs and DVDs

### How are books organized?

There are many ways to organize a lending library. Grouping books by

- genre,
- author,

- topics, or
- reading levels

are just a few of the common systems for categorizing classroom libraries. There is no one right way to categorize and organize books. The number and kinds of books in the collection, the available space, and storage options must be taken into account when determining the organization best suited for a lending library. Many teachers prefer using a combination of both color coding and sorting by book type.

**Color coding.** Morrow (2001) suggests using a color-coded system for categorizing and accessibility. For example, books about animals might be clustered together and labeled with a red sticker. Books about plants would have another color sticker and so forth. This system enables young children to find books on a topic and return them to the shelf with ease.

**Alphabetical.** Fictional picture books including traditional literature (folktales, fables, fairy tales) and realistic fiction (stories with events that could actually happen in the real world, i.e., *Amazing Grace*) could be arranged in alphabetical order, either by author or by title.

Place the books in baskets or crates with alphabet dividers. Inexpensive plastic, paddle-shaped cutting boards make excellent dividers. Other divider options include paint stirrers, heavy-duty plastic folders, and dividers from library suppliers.

All books in this section are labeled with the same color sticker. Then, if the books are filed by author, each label is marked with the initial of the author's last name. (i.e., *The Very Hungry Caterpillar* would have a C on the label because the author is Eric Carle.) Children reshelf this book behind the C marker in the book bin. This alphabetic organization enables teachers to find books quickly and encourages children to match and recognize letters and author/illustrator names.

**Topics.** Additional categories that could be used to organize the collection include:
- concepts
- songs, poems, and rhymes
- favorite characters
- science
- people and places around the world
- easy-to-read
- categories specific to children and their families, such as bilingual books, Spanish books, or an African American book collection

Each category can be labeled with a different color or shape of sticker.

Some teachers prefer to group books by topic within each of these categories. For example, concept books and books conveying specific skills can be further sorted and grouped into alphabet books, counting books, color books, shape books, number books, days of the week books, and opposites books.

Favorite character collections might be placed in a bin with accompanying puppets and toys (*Curious George, Madeline, Franklin, Froggy, Clifford, Dora*). Nonfiction science and social studies-related books might be divided into categories such as plants, animals, weather, seasons, the earth, space, dinosaurs, communities, holidays, feelings, manners, family, cultures, self, jobs/community helpers, and famous people.

### How do we manage the lending library?

*"Plan ahead or find trouble on the doorstep."*
– Confucius

Planning ahead, along with educating and empowering children and families to responsibly use library resources, are the keys to keeping a well-run lending library. Develop convenient checkout procedures, recruit and educate volunteers, and manage time to assure that books are tracked and cared for.

### How are books and activities prepared for children to take home?

Choices for parent/child home activities range from a simple book with a few activities to elaborate story bags with recordings, materials for related art projects, and recordkeeping charts.

**Include ideas for sharing books.** The most basic approach is to offer a few engaging suggestions for ways parents can interact with their children while reading the book. These guidelines can be

- printed on a large self-adhesive label and placed inside the cover of the book,
- printed on a slender piece of card stock and slipped in the book pocket, or
- laminated on a separate sheet of paper and "bagged" with the book.

Chapter 3 of this book contains guides for adult-child conversations and practical activities related to over 100 books of various genres. This resource provides a beginning point from which teachers can create their own guides for a growing library.

This approach has several benefits:

1. Only one item goes home, thus minimizing the chance of misplacing pieces.
2. Parents have convenient, step-by-step ways to share the book with their children.
3. Materials required are minimal.
4. Time required to set up and maintain the library is manageable.

**Prepare activity bags or backpacks.** Activity bags and backpacks can provide more complex take-home activities. These activity kits usually include at least some of these components

- one or several books on a topic, theme, or skill,
- laminated sheets or booklets with related parent-child activities,
- art materials or other items necessary for completing the activities, and

- recordings to accompany the books (especially beneficial for parents who do not read English or have limited reading ability themselves).

Early childhood school suppliers (see Appendix C) market individual and classroom backpack sets. Packaged backpacks are costly but require no time to assemble.

Teacher resources and downloadable parent-child activities are available from sources such as Public Television's *First Book* and Web sites for *Reading Is Fundamental* and Reading a-z (see Appendix B). These are less costly than the packaged kits. However, teachers – preferably with a cadre of volunteers – must purchase and organize the books, collect and assemble activity materials, and prepare library guidelines.

These teacher-created backpacks, a less expensive option, are very popular. They can be tailored to the particular needs of the children and their families, packaged using available materials and resources, and related to the specific curriculum being taught in the classroom. Many teachers share their original backpack ideas via their classroom and personal websites (see Appendix B).

Book backpacks and bags usually contain several books and are checked out and kept for an entire week so that families have the leisure to complete the activities over time and reread favorite stories.

**Store the bags and backpacks.** These bulky items can be challenging to display and store. Many classrooms do not have adequate space to store them attractively and in a way that is easily accessible to children. Commercially prepared bags and backpacks often can be ordered with storage racks and cubbies, but ample space is needed to set them up.

Bags and backpacks can be hung on homemade vertical coat rack hooks and hall trees, or on hanging racks purchased from school supply companies. Large plastic bins provide another storage option. Although both of these storage options are not accessible to children, teachers can take the backpacks out and put them on a table, rug, or other central area. Children then browse, select, check out, and take home the backpacks. This procedure works well for a once-a-week checkout program.

## How do I communicate with families about a lending library?

When parents are involved, starting with the initial idea and planning of any school-related activity, they are more likely to feel a sense of ownership and pride in the endeavor. If at all possible, from the beginning of the effort, involve parents in meaningful ways. Their experiences may be valuable to help make decisions about the project, choose and order books, set up the library, and continue to volunteer to maintain books and records.

Involving children in the process also can build excitement about the new resource. Children can help unpack books, glue in checkout pockets, and assist with

**Tailor backpacks to children and their families.**

When parents are involved, starting with the initial idea and planning of any school-related activity, they are more likely to feel a sense of ownership and pride in the endeavor. If at all possible, from the beginning, involve parents in meaningful ways.

similar important jobs. These experiences also are likely to lead to a greater sense of responsibility about caring for the books.

At the very least, before children choose library materials to take home, host a family meeting to share read-aloud strategies and the process for using the lending library. Successful meetings typically include food, child care, and are scheduled with parent input about the time and location.

**Hold all meetings at convenient times** when most caregivers and parents can attend. Survey families either in person, on the phone, by e-mail, or with a written questionnaire (see Appendix D for a sample). After a meeting time is established, prepare a flyer to promote the event (Appendix D includes sample flyers, agendas, and handouts). Make sure parents know about the meeting well in advance. Follow up with reminders just prior to the meeting date.

**Plan a meeting agenda.** Gather the necessary resources to build interest in the library. Checkout routines, the importance of reading with children, specific suggestions for ways to read aloud, and book care are essential elements to address.

Read a book aloud to the group, such as *Read to Your Bunny* or *Knuffle Bunny*. This is an effective way to convince parents about the importance of reading while simultaneously modeling read-aloud strategies.

**Provide food.** Breaking bread together brings people into a sense of community. Many grocery stores, restaurants, and school lunch programs will donate or prepare food for functions such as family meetings. If parents offer to provide food, encourage them to do so. Children might also be involved in the event preparation, perhaps by fixing foods described in some of their favorite books, such as *If You Give a Moose a Muffin* (Numeroff, 1991).

**Provide childcare.** Ask a colleague in another program to provide child care during the meeting. In return, offer to provide the same service during his/her parent meetings. Recruit older students or siblings to help supervise younger children. Recruit two-parent families or extended family members so one adult can help with child care while the other attends the meeting.

At the end of the gathering, thank families for coming, encourage them to volunteer if they have not already done so, and if at all possible encourage them to take home their first books immediately.

**Make sure checkout times occur routinely.**

### Implementing the System: Home and Back Again

Developing a system to check books out and back in, as well as keeping track of books read by each family, are the first steps in ensuring that books go home and return on a regular basis (Morrow, 2001).

**Set up checkout times.** Schedule checkout time whenever it works best. Some programs choose a time when volunteers are available (lunch break, between classes, during study halls in which older children are available as volunteers). Center time or just after rest time may be good choices, too. If parents come into the classroom each morning or afternoon, this may naturally be a good checkout time.

Nightly book checkout is a typical form of parent/child lending-library activity. Books are checked out at the end of a day much like a public library. Each book in the classroom library is equipped with a checkout card and pocket (see Appendix C for checkout system resources). Children select books, check them out, take them home, and return them the next day. Make sure checkout times occur routinely (daily for book packets, weekly for activity packs and backpacks).

**Checkout systems.** When possible, computerize all recordkeeping systems. Perhaps a parent or community volunteer (a savvy teenager) could set up a simple system for tracking the whereabouts of each title and which books families have read. The efficiency of such a system will make the initial investment worthwhile.

Book checkout charts can be made by gluing book checkout pockets in rows on a large piece of poster board. The chart should contain a pocket labeled with the name of each child. Charts can be laminated for durability or reinforced with clear packing tape or self-stick paper. Plastic shoe bags also serve the same purpose.

In order to check out a book, children write their names (with adult assistance as necessary) on the checkout card in the back of the book. The card is then placed in the child's pocket on the checkout chart. When the book is checked in, the child's name is crossed off, the card returned to the book pocket, and the book reshelved in the appropriate place or put in a check-in basket to be shelved at a later time.

**Travel protection.** Books and activity packets must be kept clean and dry as they travel. Some containers for this purpose that are popular and readily available include:

- large, recloseable food storage bags
- cloth bags with handles
- recycled suitcases or briefcases
- back packs
- plastic envelopes that close with a string
- laminated clasp envelopes
- clear plastic book buddy bags with handles for hanging (see Appendix C)
- sturdy cloth book bags with handles, name plate, and closures (see Appendix C)

> Volunteers can fill a wide variety of roles in the smooth functioning of a lending library. Good sources for volunteers are older students within a school, parents, grandparents, community organizations, and even the children themselves.

A laminated sheet of take-home tips and a reading record (log) should accompany every take-home book (see samples in Appendix D). Tips should include when to return the book and a few general guidelines about reading to children.

Reading logs can take many forms. Some simply have lines on which to record the title of the book and the date read. More detailed forms ask parents to respond in writing about the book-reading experience. Some teachers prefer to limit reading records to a small number of entries. Parents appreciate the simplicity, and if the record is lost or misplaced, fewer entries are lost.

**Reading incentives?** Reading is in itself one of the most intrinsically rewarding activities that children and families can share. If a program wishes to offer an incentive program intended to boost participation, planners are cautioned to carefully consider the potential short- and long-term effects on children's and parents' attitudes toward reading and their expectations for future learning experiences at home and in school.

Programs who choose to offer incentives might consider a simple technique such as encouraging families to read 100 books. Record sheets (see Appendix D for a sample) with 10 numbered lines can be used to track their progress. When 10 books are read, the child might receive a small literacy-related token (book character stickers, personal chalkboard, finger puppets, sidewalk chalk, crayons, bookmarks; see Appendix C).

Incentive charts can be used to record the number of books read. Each child's name is listed. When a child reads 10 books, a sticker is put by his or her name. The number of books read by the class can be easily totaled.

*Several notes of caution:* Many teachers find that setting up a competitive system like this detracts from children's enjoyment of books, can be seen as a burden by parents, and can even turn children away from reading. The focus may become simply on how many books are read, rather than their ultimate enjoyment. In addition, many parents do not want information about their reading successes displayed publicly. Teachers often share concerns that some children feel ostracized if they do not have as many books read to them at home as other children do. Carefully weigh the pros and cons of any reward system before implementing it.

**Involving volunteers.** Volunteers can fill a wide variety of roles in the smooth functioning of a lending library. Good sources for volunteers are older students within a school, parents, grandparents, community organizations (churches, civic organizations, Big Brothers/Big Sisters, retired teacher groups, college student groups), and even the children themselves.

Investing time up front to recruit, plan, and lead short training sessions for volunteers and staff, such as the procedures outlined in Appendix C, will yield tremendous dividends. A few agenda items to consider for a training session:

- check in/out procedures
- book repair training and materials
- reshelving routines

Classroom volunteers from community groups, family members, and/or buddy readers from upper grades can read aloud one-on-one with children.

**Time management.** Classroom teachers schedule lending library time in their daily lesson plans. Include it on all posted class schedules. When volunteers are involved,

> **Reading is an intrinsically rewarding activity for children and families.**

coordinate their schedules as well, for checkout times as well as maintenance of the books and lending system.

**How can programs ensure that books are well cared for?**

Young children are not born knowing how to use books appropriately. They must be shown. Some preschoolers may not be familiar with book-handling skills, such as how to turn the page. Every day, as books are read in the classroom, explicitly teach appropriate book care and book-handling skills (Jalongo, 2004).

When books are returned in damaged condition, remove them from the lending library. Teach children and volunteers to put books with torn covers, missing pages, and broken spines in the Book Hospital – containers designated for damaged books. Keep repair materials (clear self-stick paper, clear packing tape, duct tape, book covers) with the container. When possible, enlist children to help make repairs.

It is important to realize that books are **consumable**. A few books are likely to be lost or damaged beyond repair. The life-long readers who are formed in the process, however, make the cost well worth it!

**How can programs celebrate a successful lending library year?**

Enjoyment of reading, exposure to high-quality children's literature, and increased print awareness are the ultimate rewards for every child – so every day children engage in activities about books. These are some ways that teachers and families have culminated their joyful, shared reading experiences:

- holding a pajama party with bed-time stories
- attend a children's theater production of a favorite story
- visiting the library to sign up for library cards
- choose new books in the children's honor to add to the lending library

Ask the families and children in the program how they would like to celebrate! And involve them in the planning from start to finish.

*Choose and adapt book-related experiences to suit children's development and interests as well as goals for their learning.*

Children's Books and Related Early Literacy Activities │ Chapter 3

# Children's Books and Related Early Literacy Activities

In this book, Chapter One outlined many important reasons to read aloud to children. Chapter Two provided suggestions for partnerships that lead to effective organization of classroom libraries and home-school reading activities. This chapter suggests books that are appropriate for young children, along with simple activities for teachers and families to do with children to build literacy skills before, during, and/or after reading the books.

Fiction and classic children's literature titles are included here, and nonfiction concept books are featured. Fiction is very popular in most early childhood programs and in children's homes, while the values of nonfiction books are too often overlooked when exploring early literacy learning. It is anticipated that by emphasizing them here, educators and families alike will broaden the types of literature they read with young children.

First in this chapter, readers will find book titles listed by topics that are often part of the curriculum in classrooms with young children. An annotated list of these books is then arranged alphabetically by the author's last name. Nearly all of these books are easy to find in local libraries, bookstores, and on the Internet. Most are available in inexpensive paperback versions. Some are available in Spanish and recordings as well.

The early literacy explorations suggested here are designed to be engaging and easy to do with children. Most activities need no materials – just an adult's time, attention, and responsive conversation. Choose and adapt the book-related experiences to suit the children's development and interests as well as goals for their literacy learning. When a book is read a second and third time, adults can build on children's learning by following up with different, more in-depth literacy activities that build on their knowledge and skills.

Within each annotation, information is provided explaining the primary early literacy skills and concepts that children can develop while engaged in these learning experiences. Feel free to copy these activity sections and attach them to the inside the covers of the books as a handy reminder to encourage families to try similar learning experiences when children take the books home.

Some of the most important values of reading books to children are the interactions and conversations that take place among teachers, families, and children. These learning activities are intended to be the starting point for enjoying books together. Invent many more concrete, hands-on learning experiences that integrate curriculum standards and build on children's experiences. Scaffold their learning by picking up on the topics and vocabulary in these books and exploring them more fully. Incorporate resources in the community that build bridges between children's literacy and their everyday experiences.

## Find delightful ways to make books – and reading – come alive for children every day!

# Children's Books and Related Early Literacy Activities

## Curriculum Topics With Related Book Title

These are some of the most common topics explored with young children through projects, explorations, and hands-on activities.

A few books are suggested for each topic.

Teachers and children's librarians can identify many other titles that build on children's interests and experiences – and address the national, state, and local standards that guide curriculum development.

### Alphabet

*Alphabears: An ABC Book* (Hague)
*Clifford's ABC* (Bridwell)
*David McPhail's Animals A to Z* (McPhail)
*Eating the Alphabet: Fruits and Vegetables From A to Z* (Ehlert)
*Farm Alphabet Book* (Miller)
*From Acorn to Zoo and Everything in Between in Alphabetical Order* (Kitamura)
*Harold's ABC* (Johnson)
*On Market Street* (Lobel)

### Animals

*A House for Hermit Crab* (Carle)
*And the Cow Said Moo!* (Phillips)
*Animal Action ABC* (Pandell)
*Animal Sculpture* (Canizares & Chanko)
*Bugs* (Greenberg)
*Butterfly Alphabet* (Sandved)
*Click, Clack, Moo: Cows That Type* (Cronin)
*Cows in the Kitchen* (Crebbin)
*David McPhail's Animals A to Z* (McPhail)
*Down on the Farm* (Scelsa)
*Is Your Mama a Llama?* (Guarino)
*Over in the Meadow* (illus. by Keats)
*Swimmy* (Lionni)
*The Bear Went Over the Mountain* (adapted by Williams)
*The Little Mouse, the Red Ripe Strawberry, and the Big Hungry Bear* (Wood)
*The Mitten* (Brett)
*We're Going on a Lion Hunt* (Axtell)
*Wonderful Worms* (Glaser)

### Community Diversity

*At the Laundromat* (Loomis)
*At the Library* (Loomis)
*Bear About Town* (Blackstone)
*Chato's Kitchen* (Soto)
*In a Painting* (Canizares & Moreton)
*On Market Street* (Lobel)
*The Crocodile and the Dentist* (Gomi)

### Friends & Getting Along With Others

*Corduroy* (Freeman)
*Friends at School* (Bunnett)
*It's a Party* (Moreton & Berger)
*Jamaica Tag-Along* (Havill)
*Noisy Nora* (Wells)
*One Duck Stuck* (Root)
*Silly Sally* (Wood)
*The Day Jimmy's Boa Ate the Wash* (Noble)
*Where the Wild Things Are* (Sendak)

### Homes & Families

*A Chair for My Mother* (Williams)
*Babies* (Canizares & Chanko)
*Brothers and Sisters* (Senisi)
*Bunny Cakes* (Wells)
*Busy Toes* (Bowie)
*Families Are Different* (Pellegrini)
*Families Share* (Williams)
*How Kids Grow* (Marzollo)
*I Love You, Little One* (Trufuri)
*In the Kitchen* (Canizares & Chessen)
*Noisy Nora* (Wells)
*Read to Your Bunny* (Wells)

### Making Things

*Animal Sculpture* (Canizares & Chanko)
*Bridges* (Canizares & Moreton)
*Building Shapes* (Canizares & Berger)
*Buildings* (Chessen & Chanko)
*Clay Art With Gloria Elliot* (Chanko & Chessen)
*How to Make a Mudpie* (Williams)

### Math & Science Concepts

*26 Letters and 99 Cents* (Hoban)
*A-Counting We Will Go* (Williams)
*A House for Hermit Crab* (Carle)
*All Through the Week With Cat and Dog* (Williams)
*Bear About Town* (Blackstone)
*Bear Shadow* (Asch)
*Building Shapes* (Canizares & Berger)

*Buildings* (Chessen & Chanko)
*Cookie's Week* (Ward)
*Dinosaur Roar!* (Strickland)
*I Am Water* (Marzollo)
*I See Colors* (Williams)
*I See Shapes* (Fries)
*Inch by Inch* (Lionni)
*It's Melting!* (Williams)
*Seven Blind Mice* (Young)
*The Four Seasons* (Williams)

### Plants

*Apples* (Berger & Chessen)
*Apples and Pumpkins* (Rockwell)
*Eating the Alphabet: Fruits and Vegetables From A to Z* (Ehlert)
*Flower Garden* (Bunting)
*How Are You Peeling?* (Freymann & Elffers)
*How Do Apples Grow?* (Maestro)
*If a Tree Could Talk* (Williams)
*Red Leaf, Yellow Leaf* (Ehlert)
*The Carrot Seed* (Kraus)

### Rhyming Words & Songs

*Bugs Go Marching* (Williams)
*Five Little Monkeys Jumping on the Bed* (Christelow)
*Hush Little Baby* (illustrated by Frazee)
*I Know an Old Lady* (retold & illustrated by Karas)
*Itsy Bitsy Spider* (illustrated by Trapani)
*Over in the Meadow* (illustrated by Keats)
*The Bear Went Over the Mountain* (adapted by Williams)
*The Wheels on the Bus* (Kovalski)
*We're Going on a Lion Hunt* (Axtell)
*Who Stole the Cookies?* (Moffat)

### Self & Self-Esteem

*Amazing Grace* (Hoffman)
*Ben's Trumpet* (Isadora)
*How Are You Peeling?* (Freymann & Elffers)
*How Kids Grow* (Morzollo)
*I Can Read* (Williams)

*I Know Why I Brush My Teeth* (Rowan)
*I Love You, Little One* (Tafuri)
*Is Your Mama a Llama?* (Guarino)
*Read to Your Bunny* (Wells)

### Sorting, Classifying, & Counting

*26 Letters and 99 Cents* (Hoban)
*A-Counting We Will Go* (Williams)
*Big and Little* (Berger & Chanko)
*Bugs Go Marching* (Williams)
*Buttons, Buttons* (Williams)
*Five Little Monkeys Jumping on the Bed* (Christelow)
*How Many Can Play?* (Canizares & Chessen)
*How Many?* (Williams)
*Jamberry* (Degen)
*Over in the Meadow* (illustrated by Keats)
*Ten, Nine, Eight* (Bang)

### Stories

*Amazing Grace* (Hoffman)
*Corduroy* (Freeman)
*Flossie and the Fox* (McKissack)
*On Market Street* (Lobel)
*One Duck Stuck* (Root)
*Silly Sally* (Wood)
*The Carrot Seed* (Kraus)
*The Enormous Potato* (retold by Davis)
*The Little Red Hen* (retold by Carter)
*The Snowy Day* (Keats)
*The Three Little Pigs: An English Folktale* (retold by Sanderson)
*Where the Wild Things Are* (Sendak)

### Transportation

*First Flight* (McPhail)
*Freight Train* (Crews)
*The Wheels on the Bus* (Kovalski)

**Recommended Books and Learning Experiences**

Children's Books and Related Early Literacy Activities

## Bear Shadow

by Frank Asch                                                       Scholastic, 1990

- **Explore physics.** Asch portrays an interesting way for young children to explore a significant physical science concept – when an object blocks light, a shadow is formed. Find out what children know about shadows from their own experience. Books are sources of interesting ideas.

- **Catch shadows.** On a sunny day, go outside and ask children to find their shadows. Watch how shadows change when children move in different ways. Mark the sizes and shapes of shadows with chalk or tape. Go back a few hours later and note how shadows changed over time. Children observe and record changes in the world around them that are related to the books they read.

- **Play Shadow Tag together.** Simplify the rules as needed. Make sure all children who wish can participate. Keep the game friendly rather than competitive. Reading and books can lead to fun physical activities.

- **Make shadow portraits.** Ask child to sit or stand near a wall on which a large paper is taped. One person shines the flashlight on the child's head. Another traces the outline of the shadow with a pencil or crayon on the paper. Children cut or tear out their profiles and attach them to dark paper. Or suggest they color the picture, adding detailed facial features. Hands-on art experiences enable children to express what they are learning with written symbols.

## We're Going on a Lion Hunt

by David Axtell                                                      Scholastic, 2001

- **Read and repeat.** In this version of the traditional story chant, two sisters go looking for a lion. The story filled with repetition, giving children opportunities to "read" along with the words as soon as they have heard a few pages. Participating while an adult reads builds children's confidence that they are readers, too.

- **Act out concepts.** When the girls meet each obstacle, they "Can't go over it; under it; around it; or through it." The book gives many opportunities to demonstrate the meaning of these important prepositions in a fun and meaningful context. Use a blanket or furniture such as a table to act out the concepts. Reading builds vocabulary and the ability to figure out word meaning from the context of text and illustrations.

- **Go on a lion hunt.** With children, make up rules to hold a lion hunt, indoors or out. Ask children to suggest other animal names for the hunt. Books can lead to fun physical activities.

## Ten, Nine, Eight

by Molly Bang                                                        Scholastic, 1983

- **Share bedtime rituals.** Children are usually eager to tell about their bedtime routines.

- **What do they do to get ready for bed?** Use a language experience chart to record what each child says. (Todd said, "I always wear my green jammies." Make a simple graph to show bedtimes. Stories have meaning in people's lives. Everyone has stories to tell.

- **Fill in the rhyme!** This story is told through a series of rhyming couplets. Most of the rhyming words have the same rime (snow:row; down:gown; close:nose). Others do not (bed:head). After hearing the book one time, see if children can fill in the rhyming words. Participating while an adult reads builds children's confidence that they are readers, too. Children listen more carefully when they have something specific for which to listen.

- **Find the look-alikes.** Point out how many rhyming words sound alike and look alike at the ends. (Be sure not to use bed:head as an example because it is an exception.) Alphabet letters and language sounds are related.

## *The Mitten*

by Jan Brett                                                                                       Scholastic, 1990

- **Predict what will happen next.** *The Mitten* is one of many beautifully illustrated books by Brett. This one retells a Ukrainian folktale. The story structure makes it a great opportunity for children to make predictions about what will happen next and how the problem of the lost mitten will be solved. Authors use many different ways to tell their stories.

- **What would you do?** Ask children to imagine that they face other common dilemmas. How would they solve the problem? Book characters solve problems.

- **Make mittens!** Children place their open palms on paper and trace around each other's hands with markers or crayons. Children decorate their hands as if they were wearing mittens. Older children may want to add borders on the page, much like those in the book. Hands-on art experiences enable children to express what they are learning with written symbols.

## *Clifford's ABC*

by Norman Bridwell                                                                              Scholastic, 1983

- **Match words and pictures.** Ask children to name and describe the pictures on each page. Point out that each picture has a word label. Words can be spoken, written, and illustrated.

- **What does it mean?** What is it? Explain the meanings of unfamiliar words. Relate ideas to children's everyday experiences. Show pictures or find real examples at home or school. When children understand spoken words, it is easier for them to learn to read them.

- **Find first letters.** All words on a page start with a featured letter. Ask a child to point to all of the C's (or other letters) on the page. Recognizing alphabet letters, and their place in words, helps children learn to identify words and sounds of letters.

- **Listen for same first sounds.** All words on a page begin with the same letter, and most begin with the same sound. As objects on a page are named, talk about how they sound alike at the beginning. Being able to hear the similarities in spoken words is important to

*Note: Books are listed alphabetically by the first author's last name.*

**Recommended Books and Learning Experiences**

### Children's Books and Related Early Literacy Activities

understand how speaking and writing are related. Words that sound alike often have the same letters.

- **Match picture labels to words.** The words that appear as picture labels are listed on the sides of the page. A more advanced activity is to find the picture labels that match the words on the list. Words can be illustrated with pictures.

## *Apples*

by Samantha Berger & Betsy Chessen                         Scholastic, 1998

- **Count!** Together, count the apples in each picture as the child points to them. Then ask the child to count alone. Use prompts as needed, such as, "What comes after 4? Let's see, 1, 2, 3, 4…" Numbers are represented by words. Things can be counted with words.

- **Get to know the authors and illustrators.** On the last 2 pages of the book, the authors tell something interesting about each picture or artist. Talk about the pictures and the stories behind them. New vocabulary possibilities include round, beach, Mexico, colors, pitcher, fruit, cloth. Books are written and illustrated by people. The people and their pictures have interesting stories to tell.

- **Tell new stories.** With children, make up a story about the apples and the people in each picture. "Why do you think the apples are there? What are the people going to do with the apples?" Stories have structure: characters, action, and setting.

- **Read the pictures.** Next book-sharing time, ask children to tell the story about one or two of the pictures. Repeating stories in their own words helps children remember words and ideas.

## *Big and Little*

by Samantha Berger & Pamela Chanko                         Scholastic, 1999

- **Point out the words.** Use a finger to point to the words as you read. Spoken words match written words one-to-one. Print is what the reader reads. Readers look at the print from left to right.

- **Hunt for big and little.** Find big and little things indoors and outdoors (big chair and little chair; big box and little box). Words can be used to compare similarities and differences in things.

- **Explore more.** The last two pages of this book give much information about the objects in the pictures. Share some of this information before, during, or after reading the book. Relate the objects to ones with which children are familiar. Encourage children to ask questions. Talking about interesting ideas encourages children to look forward to reading. They remember better because they listen well. Asking questions is an important skill for life-long learning.

# Chapter 3

### *Bear About Town*

by Stella Blackstone      Illustrated by Debbie Harter      Scholastic, no date

- **Read with rhyme.** Read the story first, emphasizing the rhyming words. The next time or two, ask children to fill in the rhyming words. Hearing rhymes helps children associate letters with sounds.

- **What day is it?** Read the story, emphasizing the days of the week. Find those words in other places (calendars, newspaper date lines). Children are eager to learn to recognize a few important and useful words. Knowing a few words helps them learn other words.

- **Explore maps.** At the end of the story is a map of all the places Bear went. With children, match the places on the map to the pages in the story. Later, go outdoors to look at street signs and talk about the words on them. Check out blueprints and local maps to identify familiar places. Together, draw a map of the classroom, building, or neighborhood. Use words to label the places. Create 3-D maps with blocks or recycled boxes. Reading is useful. Words and drawings can represent places.

### *Busy Toes*

by C.W. Bowie      illustrated by Fred Willingham      Scholastic, 1998

- **Get tickled by toes!** Enjoy all the funny and interesting things that Bowie thought of to do with toes! Laugh with children about the funny things. If you have ever done any of these things with your toes, talk about it as you read. If not, try them together! Books are sources of interesting ideas. Reading can lead to fun physical activities.

- **Try out new words.** Explain some of the interesting words (squishing, tippy, cuddling) with familiar words. With children, play a variation of Simon Says to imitate the actions described. Words are fun to play with!

- **Tickle your tongues!** Some of these words are just plain fun to say! Repeat some of the interesting words or read along and then wait for children to fill in the fun words. Being delighted by words makes learning new words fun.

### *Friends at School*

by Rochelle Bunnett      photographs by Matt Brown      Scholastic, 1995

- **Relate the book to real people.** Before reading this book, talk about school. "Who are your friends at school? What do you and your friends like to do together?" Books can be about people just like us.

- **What's happening?** After reading the book, look back at the pictures. Encourage children to talk about the things children in the book are doing that are like the things they do at school. Books help children recall details about people, sequences of events, and reflect on places they know.

- **Share a memory.** Talk about the things that you remember doing in preschool or kindergarten. Tell children about your best school friends and the activities you enjoyed together. Stories have meaning to our lives. They are not just things that happen to other people.

*Note: Books are listed alphabetically by the first author's last name.*

**Recommended Books and Learning Experiences**

## Children's Books and Related Early Literacy Activities

### *Flower Garden*

by Eve Bunting     illustrated by Katheryn Hewitt     Scholastic, 1994

- **Plan a surprise.** In the story, a girl and her Dad make a special surprise for Mom. Together, talk about memories of children's surprises, birthdays, or special presents. What new surprises could the children make happen? Stories give us good ideas about how to treat people.

- **Explore flowers.** The girl and her Dad buy flowers and make a window box for Mom. Explain some of the unfamiliar words (trowel, potting soil, potting mix, jamboree) by showing the real items. Ask "Who knows what this garden tool is called?" While reading, point to and name the flowers (pansies, daisies, daffodils, geraniums, tulips). Visit a garden center and find the same flowers. If possible, grow flowers for all to care for and enjoy! Words in books describe real things people can find out more about.

- **Wait for a response.** The story uses many rhyming words. When reading the book a second time, pause to give children time to say the rhyming word (great/wait; bus/us; floor/door; street/meet; see/jamboree; too/you). Being able to hear the similarities in spoken words is important to understand how speaking and writing are related. Words that sound alike often have the same letters.

### *Animal Sculpture*

by Susan Canizares & Pamela Chanko     Scholastic, 1999

- **Read separate words.** With a finger or bookmark, point just under the words as they are said. Sometimes, use palms to block out the words around one word, and focus on just that word. Say the letters together. Spoken words match written words one-to-one.

- **Get to know the words.** Pick out the new vocabulary words: quarry, metal, ladybug, pipe, torch, weld, anonymous, boards, sculpture, festival, lobster, origami, recycle. Find ways to relate each word to something familiar in the everyday world. It's fun to discover new words and relate them to familiar things.

- **Sculpt!** On the last 2 pages of the book, the authors tell about how the artist made each sculpture. While reading the book, or after, tell something interesting about the sculptures. Go on a sculpture hunt to find sculptures outdoors and inside. Make sculptures with modeling compound, or glue recycled materials together. Books are sources of new ideas to try. They encourage people to notice things all around.

- **Match the animal names.** After reading the book, look back at the pictures and ask children to name the animal on each page. Point to the word on the page that tells the animal's name as the child says the name. Animals have names – sometimes several different ones. Words that are spoken can be written.

### *Babies*

by Susan Canizares & Pamela Chanko     Scholastic, 1999

- **Fill in the words.** After the first page, each page repeats the phrase, "Babies need…." Soon, children can predict the word by looking at the picture. Reading contains messages that make sense. People use what they already know to figure out how to read a word.

- **Talk about babies.** Make a list of what children know about taking care of babies. The last two pages of this book give information about taking care of babies. What other things are on the list? Add them to the children's list. Books can add to what people already know about something very familiar.

- **Remember when…** Share stories about taking care of babies. Encourage children to share their own baby pictures. Discussing compelling personal stories helps children relate reading to their own lives.

## *Building Shapes*

by Susan Canizares & Samantha Berger                                    Scholastic, 1999

- **Explain the shapes.** While reading, point out features of each shape and trace the sides with a finger. "See how the triangle has three sides. One, two, three. That's how you know it's a triangle." When children understand spoken words, it is easier for them to learn to read them.

- **Build on repetition.** After the first page of this book, each page repeats the phrase, "Buildings are (name of shape)…" This repetition helps children to read along after hearing the story. Read it again later. Messages we read make sense. Often you can use something you already know to figure out how to read a word.

- **Explore buildings.** The last 2 pages of this book provide information about the buildings in the pictures. Share the information. Relate it to buildings children already know. The next time the book is read, ask children to find these buildings. Children listen more carefully when they have something specific to find.

- **Find more shapes.** After reading this book, see what shapes children can find in their homes or neighborhood. Go on a shape treasure hunt. Sketch or take pictures of the shapes. Reading makes sense when children can see its relationship to their own lives.

## *Bridges*

by Susan Canizares & Daniel Moreton                                    Scholastic, 1999

- **Feel new words.** Explain new words such as narrow or curved with gestures. Use familiar items such as unit blocks to demonstrate their meanings. Ask children to use these words to describe things they know. "What else do you know that is curved?" When children understand spoken words, it is easier for them to learn to read them.

- **Anticipate what comes next.** After the first page, each page repeats the phrase, "This bridge is…" This repetition will make it easy for children to "read" along after hearing the story. Sometimes, just for fun, finish the sentence with something different! Reading makes sense. Readers can find patterns in how authors write their books.

- **Learn more about bridges.** The last 2 pages provide facts about the bridges in the book's pictures. Point out highlights. Together, find pictures of similar bridges. Talk about their similarities and differences. Talking about illustrations, and using words in context, helps children understand how they can gain more information from books.

*Note:
Books are listed alphabetically by the first author's last name.*

**Recommended Books and Learning Experiences**

## Children's Books and Related Early Literacy Activities

- **Look for more bridges.** Are there any bridges in the area? What words describe them? (tall, straight, narrow, wide, concrete, steel). If possible, take pictures or make sketches of some of the bridges. Look for shapes and visual vocabulary in their construction (arches, triangles, straight lines, curved lines). Ask children to notice details. "Who or what uses the bridges (people, cars, trains)?" Count traffic to see how busy the bridges are. Books can lead to many more exciting learning experiences.

### *How Many Can Play?*
Susan Canizares & Betsey ChessenScholastic, 1999

- **Follow with a finger.** Point to the words while reading them. Moving smoothly doesn't help learning 1-to-1 voice/print match. Spoken words match written words one-to-one. Print is what readers read. Readers look at the print from left to right.

- **Count and match.** On many pages, a number word (one, two, three) is featured. When reading the book a second time, pause and let children say the number word. Together, count the children in the picture to figure out the word. When children say the number, point out the number word. Write the numerals in the air with arms, or form them with bodies (one or more). Words are useful for solving problems. Knowing a few words leads to learning other words. Sometimes new words can be figured out by thinking about what makes sense.

- **Play games.** Read more about the games children play in the book. Adapt and play them with children, indoors and out. Invent your own games, too. Books give people new ideas for having fun together.

### *In a Painting*
by Susan Canizares & Daniel MoretonScholastic, 1999

- **Describe the picture.** Suggest that children find the object in the picture that the words describe (red fish, orange windows). Encourage them to use adjectives such as colors and shapes to tell about the items. Paying close attention to illustrations helps children become more observant of detail, an important skill for learning to read.

- **Find color words.** When reading the book a second time, show children the color words in the text. Find these colors in the clothes they are wearing, the room around them, and other places. Offer these colors for painting or fingerpainting. Some words describe details about things. These words are specific and people all know what they mean.

- **Explore fine art.** At the end of the book, the author provides more information about the paintings and the artists. What media did the artists use? Do their paintings look realistic or are they abstract? Ask children to use descriptive words for each painting. Show children how to use similar art techniques as they paint. When children gain experience with art media, they better appreciate how illustrations add to the meaning and richness of a book's message. Meaning can be expressed with symbols and words.

# Chapter 3

## *In the Kitchen*

by Susan Canizares & Betsey Chessen　　　　　　　　　　　　　　Scholastic, 1999

- **Follow left to right.** Move a hand or bookmark from left to right along with the words while reading. In English, words are read from left to right, top to bottom.

- **Cook in the kitchen!** Read more about the cooking process that is featured on each page. Explore a variety of recipe books and cards for children's favorite foods. Make shopping lists. Shop together and find the ingredients. Cook together, making sure children help read the recipe, measure ingredients, stir mixtures, set timers, and are safely involved in all aspects of food preparation. Words are good reminders for daily tasks. Books give people new ideas and help them follow directions.

## *A House for Hermit Crab*

by Eric Carle　　　　　　　　　　　　　　　　　　　　　　　　Scholastic, 1987

- **Build vocabulary.** This story is filled with rich, descriptive vocabulary (frightening, attack, wriggling/wraggling, flock, decorate, debris), as well as the months of the year and names of many ocean animals. With each reading, focus on something different! Books can be appreciated for many things – new vocabulary words, how time is organized, and information about the world. Readers find new and different things each time they read a book!

- **Find the problem.** Hermit Crab has a problem to solve and meets characters along the way. After enjoying the story, talk with children about what the problem was and how it was solved. When reading other stories, use this skill to identify problem in those books as well. Stories have elements in common. When readers know the elements and how they work together, they can make good predictions about the stories.

- **What's the message?** The story also has a message about embracing change as an adventure rather than as something to fear. What message do children think that Eric Carle is giving when he tells Hermit Crab's story? Look for messages in other familiar books as well. There may be several, and each person may find a unique message! Every author has a message. Sometimes people get different messages from the same story.

## *The Little Red Hen, An English Folktale in Two Versions*

retold by Jackie Carter　　　　　　　　　　　　　　　　　　　　Rigby, 2003

- **Read BIG!** This version of an old favorite has large print that makes details easy for a small group of children to see. Ask children to help hold the book and turn the pages. Make them part of the entire reading experience. Children who are involved in handling books learn first-hand how to treat books.

- **Repeat!** After hearing the book a few times, children enjoy reading the repetitive lines: "Not I," said the duck (cat, pig). Say the lines with different voices and in different pitches to give each character personality. Children pay close attention when they know they have a role in the telling of the story. Characters speak in different voice tones.

*Note: Books are listed alphabetically by the first author's last name.*

**Recommended Books and Learning Experiences**

## Children's Books and Related Early Literacy Activities

- **Pick out important words.** The book's clear print and matching pictures help children begin to recognize the animal words. Point them out. Then ask children to find them. Young readers soon can identify familiar words. This helps them learn other, similar words.

- **Do a short play.** At the end of the book is a short play that identifies the characters and their lines with pictures. With children, create simple costumes or puppets. Rearrange furniture and use blankets, boxes, or other items to decorate sets. Perform the play for each other. Words that can be read can also be spoken. Real people or puppets can represent characters.

### *Clay Art With Gloria Elliot*

by Pamela Chanko & Betsey Chessen          Scholastic, 1999

- **Incorporate artists' tools.** Use a modeling tool such as a craft stick or paintbrush to point to the words while reading. Readers have different ways to keep their place in the text. Artists use tools, too, to make their illustrations.

- **Sculpt with modeling compounds.** Read about how Elliot makes her beautiful objects from clay. Compare different types of clay with other modeling compounds. "How do they feel? Smell? How long do they need to dry? How messy are they? What colors are they?" Explore the possibilities of sculpture with a variety of modeling compounds on different days. Show children simple modeling techniques such as making slabs (roll or press out by hand), pinching (squeezing bits of compound to make details), and imprinting (pressing items into the compound to leave textures). People have a variety of talents that can be described in words and pictures. Reading leads from one new interesting experience to another.

### *Buildings*

by Betsey Chessen & Pamela Chanko          Scholastic, 1998

- **What are buildings made of?** After the first page, each page repeats the phrase, "Some are made of…" Identify the materials by feeling real-life samples. Walk in the neighborhood to find different types of building materials. Messages in words and pictures make sense. These messages lead to learning more about the world and how things work.

- **What's under construction?** After reading this book and exploring the neighborhood, look for buildings that are under construction. If possible, talk with workers about their jobs, from architect to carpenter to truck driver. Look at blueprints. Identify construction materials. Sketch and photograph each stage of the building process. Display the children's illustrations along with their captions describing the construction, or make a class book about the project. Words and pictures help construction workers do their jobs. Words help describe exactly how something happens.

## *Five Little Monkeys Jumping on the Bed*

by Eileen Christelow                              Scholastic, 1989

- **What would happen?** Introduce the book by asking questions such as, "What would happen if you jumped on the bed? Why would you get in trouble if you jumped on the bed?" Stories can describe ideas that may not be good to actually do. People choose whether the stories show people at their best behavior.

- **Build on the momentum.** After the first sequence of events (jumping on the bed, falling off, and bumping heads), the story repeats. Children enjoy joining in the repeat with the reader. Books sometimes have patterns that help readers know what to expect next. Knowing these patterns helps readers figure out the words

- **Pick out ending words.** When reading the story a second time, point out the word bed, which occurs at the end of the line on several pages. Point to it and pause so children can say (read) it. Encourage children to find it on the pages, too. Write the word on other surfaces such as paper, chalkboards, and dry-erase boards. Label any beds in the classroom (doll beds, flower beds). Words look the same each time they are repeated.

## *Cows in the Kitchen*

by June Crebbin        illustrated by Katharine McEwen        Scholastic, 1998

- **Read along.** On facing pages of this book, the text is almost the same. After reading the story one time, reread it and encourage children to pick up on the pattern by reading along. Books can be predictable. Readers figure out what is the same and what changes on each page.

- **Learn animal words.** Point out the animal words on each page (cows, ducks, pigs, hens, sheep). If possible, visit farms or at least see videos with these animals so children get a sense of their sizes, shapes, sounds, and smells. Play singing games such as "Old MacDonald." All animals have names (and some have many different names). Words are just the beginning for finding information about creatures.

- **Try out new words.** Some words in the story may be unfamiliar (haystack, armchair, latch, creep). Explain them while enjoying the story, in context, and with the illustrations as a guide. When possible, demonstrate or show real items, such as a bunch of hay. Creep quietly around the room. Latch a gate. Make the words come to life! Vocabulary words are fun to say and figure out. People use lots of different clues to understand words.

## *Freight Train*

by Donald Crews                              Scholastic, 1978

- **Which color is each car?** The cars of the freight train are different colors, and the text describing each car is printed in the same color. For example, the word red is printed in red. Ask children if they notice any changes from page to page. Encourage children to make drawings of things using colors in a similar way. Authors and illustrators give readers lots of ways to figure out the meaning of text.

- **Find the spaces.** The text is large and simple, making it easy to see the words and how they are separated with white space. Ask children to place a finger each time they see a

*Note: Books are listed alphabetically by the first author's last name.*

**Recommended Books and Learning Experiences**

space between words. What is the word between the spaces? There are spaces between each word. Look carefully at each page and each word!

- **Listen and look for local trains.** Explore different types of trains, such as subways, passenger trains, high-speed trains, freight trains, and monorails. Compare pictures of each to find out how they are different and the same. If possible, watch trains as they move. What is their cargo? Listen for the sounds when they approach an intersection or depot. Why are trains an important way to transport people and things? Use recycled boxes, a few chairs, and small pieces of paper (tickets) to encourage pretend train play. Books can lead to lots of interesting experiences.

## *Click, Clack, Moo: Cows That Type*

by Doreen Cronin      pictures by Betsy Lewin      Scholastic, 2000

- **Write notes! In this funny story,** the animals get what they want from the farmer by writing notes to him on an old typewriter. After enjoying the story together, write children notes on scrap paper. Write something simple and meaningful such as "I love you!" Encourage them to write back! Writing is an important way to communicate ideas.

- **Type, too!** If possible, find an old typewriter. Compare it to a computer. Encourage children to write notes to each other or people they love with markers, typewriters, and computers (scribbles, drawings, invented spellings – they all communicate!). Ask children to read their notes to the recipients. Messages can be communicated in many forms. Everyone loves to get messages!

## *The Enormous Potato*

retold by Aubrey Davis      illustrated by Dusan Petricic      Scholastic, 1997

- **Explore potatoes!** Before reading this book, check out some potatoes. Who knows how new potato plants grow? Find the eyes and sprouts growing from them. Wash and smell freshly cut potatoes. If possible, visit a farm where potatoes are growing. Where are the potatoes? Books can be about things people already know, or about things yet to be discovered.

- **Read along!** The story has a repeated section that builds as the story goes along ("The daughter grabbed the wife. The wife grabbed the farmer. The farmer grabbed the potato.") After the first few pages, children enjoy saying the repeat. When children identify the pattern and read long, they gain confidence in exploring books.

- **Listen to answer questions.** After reading the story, ask, "Who was the helper who finally got the potato to come out?" Look back in the book to find out. Was it the biggest helper? Talk about ways that children help to make a difference in getting a big job done. Readers can reread sections of books to find answers to questions.

- **Keep investigating potatoes!** As a follow up to the book, read and follow recipes to prepare and taste potatoes in different forms (potato salad, baked, fries, whipped, latkes). Grow a potato! Even a simple idea can be explored in depth through reading!

## *Jamberry*

by Bruce Degen                                         Scholastic, 1990

- **Invent silly rhymes!** This fantastically silly rhyming story is accompanied by pictures that tell an even wilder tale. The rhyme is infectious and after hearing it a few times, children enjoy reading along. The fun of reading is contagious! All ages can enjoy books. Reading is meant to be shared with friends and family.

- **Try out new words.** Some of the unfamiliar words (such as "razzamatazzberry") are just for fun. Come up with other silly words that combine sounds and ideas. Feel them tickle on tongues and on lips. Write them down so they're not forgotten. With children, invent a new story with the new words. Illustrate it with children's art. Language is always changing. Words are fun to play with.

- **Get into jam!** What a good opportunity to talk about jam and different types of berries or other fruits that are used to make jam. Taste jam on toast, jam on crackers, jam on apple slices, and jam on yogurt. If possible, ask someone to talk about and demonstrate how jam is made. Read labels on containers of jam. What are the ingredients? Words describe everyday experiences and help people decide what to buy and eat.

## *Eating the Alphabet: Fruits & Vegetables From A to Z*

by Lois Ehlert                                         Scholastic, 1989

- **Touch and taste!** The beautiful illustrations in this book show both common and unusual fruits and vegetables. Use the book to introduce or follow up with a trip to a grocery store, farmer's market, orchard, or produce farm. Make a list of what fruits and vegetables to look for. Children wash, use plastic utensils to cut, and taste as many as possible. Words are useful to remember things.

- **Upper- or lower-case letters?** Ehlert uses both capital (upper-) and lower-case letters for the names of fruits and vegetables. Point out that all letters have two forms. Look at children's names, ads in magazines, and other print to find both types of letters. Words have both capital and lowercase letters. They sound and mean the same. Some words always begin with capital letters. Knowing that there are two forms helps beginning readers keep from becoming confused.

- **Pick out important letters.** Find all the B's and all the b's, for example, in children's names. Count how many of each type of letters they found. What other words do children know that begin with these letters? Children often notice the letters in their names first. Build on what they already know to broaden their awareness of letters – an important step in learning to read.

## *Red Leaf, Yellow Leaf*

by Lois Ehlert                                         Scholastic, 1999

- **Learn the language of botany.** This book combines elements of both fiction and nonfiction while describing how a tree grows from a seed. Many science concepts are explored, and the book is filled with interesting vocabulary (twirled, whirled, among,

*Note:
Books are listed alphabetically by the first author's last name.*

## Children's Books and Related Early Literacy Activities

**Recommended Books and Learning Experiences**

nursery, transplanted, uprooted) to discuss and even act out – twirl and whirl! When children understand spoken words, it is easier to learn to read them.

- **Get to know leaves.** At any season, look at the different shapes and colors of leaves. Watch leaves as they emerge in the spring. Tear jagged leaf shapes from paper and color them. Make crayon rubbings of leaves (place leaf with veins up, cover with paper, rub with the side of an unwrapped crayon). Make collages with colorful fall leaves. Label leaves from different types of trees. Ideas from books last for all seasons. Books help people look more closely at nature.

- **Study the spaces.** The print is large in this book, and the spacing between words makes it a good choice for pointing one-to-one and showing how words are made of letters with spaces between. Groups of letters make words. Space between words helps people read each word separately.

### Corduroy
by Don Freeman                                                                                  Scholastic, 1968

- **Identify problems to solve.** This satisfying story addresses themes of friendship and the need to belong in ways that young children can understand. A stuffed bear who wants a home and a little girl who want a bear both overcome obstacles so they can be together. Ask children to think: "How did they solve the problem? How would you solve the problem?" With similar books, help children figure out what the problem is that the characters are trying to solve. Books give people good ideas about figuring out life and how to make it friendlier for everyone.

- **Anticipate!** The story lends itself very well to stopping and asking children what they think will happen next. After the first reading, when children know what happened, ask them to think about what else MIGHT have happened. Act out alternate endings. Stories have many elements in common and authors make lots of choices when they write them. There are many ways that stories could end.

- **Dig deeply for meaning.** The classic elements of story (character, setting, problems, solution, deeper meaning or theme) are easy to identify. Engage in interesting discussions to find out what children are thinking after they have heard the story. Children's reactions to books help adults understand their perspectives. Use these understandings to build new learning experiences through reading and hands-on activities.

### How Are You Peeling? Foods With Moods
by Saxton Freymann & Joost Elffers                                                         Scholastic, no date

- **Get in the mood!** This book uses strange-looking fruits and vegetables to illustrate many different emotions. While reading, help children use these illustrations to figure out the meanings of new words, or words that are used in new ways (blue, grumpy, secure, amused, frustrated, timid, ashamed, embarrassed, jealous, disappointed, wired). Words can have many different meanings. Words help people describe how they feel.

- **Explore feelings.** Talk with children about the emotions that are illustrated. Relate the feelings to times children have felt that emotion – or its opposite. Create puppets with facial expressions that express emotions. Paper plates and lunch bags make great puppet faces. Authors and illustrators of books understand how readers feel – and they connect their stories with real people and what happens in their lives.

## *I See Shapes*

by Marcia Fries                                                                               Creative Teaching Press, 1995

illustrated by students in the multi-age primary school
at Lee School in Los Alamitos, California

- **Children can illustrate books, too!** Make sure children are aware of how the illustrations came about for this book. Encourage them to write and illustrate their own simple books. Fold sheets of paper in half, make accordion folds, tape several sheets together for a scroll, or use notebooks in which children dictate or write their own stories. Encourage young authors and illustrators to tell their stories! Everyone has stories to tell. People can write and illustrate books at any age! Books come in many different forms.

- **Trace and say the shapes.** Ask children to trace the outlines of 2-D shapes with their fingers while saying the shape name. Talk about the characteristics of each shape. "Circles are round and round. Rectangles have two long sides and two shorter sides." Find the related 3-D shapes, too, such as balls and blocks. Words mean more when children touch them, say them, and see them in print.

- **Search for shapes.** Look for objects with similar shapes, indoors and out. Sketch each one. Label it with the name of the shape. Who can find things that combine two or more shapes? When children apply what they learn from listening, the words will be learned more readily when they are seen in print.

- **Identify mystery shapes.** Trace other illustrations and objects (hats, presents, birthday cake) to identify their shapes and forms. Try feeling for safe objects (sponges, spoons, blocks) inside a pillowcase without peeking. Who can identify the mystery shapes? Write the names of each object. Ask children to explain what clues made it possible for them to identify the object (cold, soft, square). When all of children's senses are engaged in the reading process, they are more likely to remember what they learn.

## *Wonderful Worms*

by Linda Glaser                                                                                                Scholastic, 1992

- **Explore the world of worms.** This book is filled with fascinating facts about earthworms, and the last two pages provide answers to additional questions that children may ask. The beautiful illustrations offer even more information about woodland creatures. Ask a gardener to talk about and show worms in soil.

- **Create "worm" spatter paintings.** Tear and twist pieces of recycled newspaper into worm shapes. Lay them on paper in an interesting design. Spatter paint over the top. Remove the papers to see the crawling worms! Why not give a name to each of the worms, or write a story about their adventures? Ideas from reading can be expressed not only in words but in creative pictures, too.

*Note:
Books are listed alphabetically by the first author's last name.*

**Recommended Books and Learning Experiences**

Children's Books and Related Early Literacy Activities

## *The Crocodile and the Dentist*

by Taro Gomi                                                                                  Scholastic, 1996

- **What's the message?** Before reading this story, find out what children already know about the dentist and about crocodiles. Fill in any gaps, so that the story makes sense. The crocodile doesn't want to go to the dentist, and the dentist doesn't really want to have the crocodile for a patient. Talk about what is happening on each page and why each character is afraid. Stories make more sense when people already know something about the situations and characters. Sometimes the message in a book is revealed in its illustrations as well as with the words.

- **Focus on dental health.** Make sure all children have regular dental checkups. Invite a dentist or dental hygienist to talk with the children about what happens at the dentist. How can they take good care of their teeth? What will happen to the baby teeth? If possible, in small groups visit a dental office, sit in the chair, and look at X-rays and impressions of teeth. Explore the unusual sights and sounds. Offer some simple props for children to pretend to play dentist office. Books can help people learn more about how to stay healthy and take good care of their bodies.

- **Write dentist stories.** Ask children to invent their own dentist stories about other animals or people they know who have had fillings, braces, false teeth, implants, or other dental procedures. Practice good dental hygiene by "brushing the teeth" of stuffed animals and dolls. Together, write and illustrate a reassuring book about a visit to the dentist to share with other children. Stories have meaning to our own lives. They are not just things that happen to other people.

---

## *Bugs*

by David T. Greenberg            illustrated by Lynn Munsinger            Scholastic, 1997

- **Laugh and listen!** Enjoy this silly and sometimes disgusting rhyme about bugs. Laugh (and gag) with the children while looking at and talking about the pictures. Humor is a great way to keep children interested in any topic! When children are good listeners and are curious (ask lots of questions) they are likely to become good readers.

- **Create a vocabulary treasure hunt.** Besides the names of the bugs, the rhyme has many interesting words (glaring, pincers, fiercer, infestin', loathe, hunch, squirt, intuition, nifty, microscopic, udder, fetch, incandescent, larvae, brooch, navel, trampolines, culinary, bodacious, phenomenal, whirligigs, nibble). Look at the pictures for clues. What other words help readers know about the meaning of unfamiliar words? Use a children's dictionary. Interview other people to find out what words mean. Go beyond offering explanations to make each word into a treasure hunt! It's fun to figure out what new words mean and how to say them. Readers have many different ways to learn new vocabulary.

# Chapter 3

## *Is Your Mama a Llama?*

by Deborah Guarino                                                   Scholastic, 1989

- **Find the rhymes and rimes.** In this rhyming story, a young llama asks his animal friends if their mamas are llamas, too. Children are delighted by the playful rhymes. Find the rhyming words and look at their endings. Some have the same letters (rime) and some do not. The English language is full of interesting surprises. The more words people know, the more mysteries there seem to be.

- **Meet the animals.** Animal words are written in large print, and the rhyme provides an interesting fact about each animal's habitat. Learn more about each animal, such as the names of their young, how many babies they have, and what they eat. Animals are often the subjects of books, both fiction and nonfiction. The more children know about the characters, the more interesting the stories become.

## *Alphabears: An ABC Book*

by Kathleen Hague          illustrated by Michael Hague          Scholastic, 1992

- **Savor new words.** Before, during, and/or after reading, talk about unfamiliar words (snuggle, stuffy, bow tie, flop, jungle, frightful, gruff, beware, hot cakes, fair, mysterious, quilted, mittens, vet, soars). Find examples that are similar (pancakes), read books using the word in another context (*The Mitten*), and even act out the verbs (flop, soars). Words that children understand from personal experience are much easier to learn to read.

- **Invent new rhymes!** After enjoying the book, make up rhymes with children's names. Example: J is for Jeremy who loves to jump. Better watch out or he'll give you a bump! Learning letters often begins with recognizing the first letter in a child's own name.

- **Create a rhyme book.** Write down the rhymes children invent. Children illustrate their own work. Punch holes and bind the book together with yarn or ribbon. Words that can be spoken can be written. Book illustrations show what the written words describe.

## *Jamaica Tag-Along*

by Juanita Havill                                                        Scholastic, 1991

- **Talk about families.** Jamaica has a problem with her older brother, Ossie. Through her experience with a younger child, a solution is found. Ask children to think about times they have had problems with their brothers or sisters. How did they find a solution? Books sometimes describe situations that many people can recognize. Stories can give us ideas about how to get along better with each other.

- **Identify story elements.** Story elements are easy to identify in this heartwarming story (characters, setting, problem, solution, deeper meaning or message). After sharing and enjoying the story, discuss the elements, one at a time with repeated readings. Find other stories with similarities. Most stories have elements in common. When readers reflect on the elements, the story becomes even more interesting.

*Note: Books are listed alphabetically by the first author's last name.*

# Children's Books and Related Early Literacy Activities

**Recommended Books and Learning Experiences**

## *Hush, Little Baby*
folk song with pictures by Marla Frazee  Scholastic, 1999

- **Concentrate on the cover.** Read the title of the book and talk about the picture on the cover. "What is the little girl trying to do? What do you think the story will be about?" When children are prepared to listen and anticipate what might happen, they are more likely to pay attention to details in the book.

- **Follow the sentences.** Move a finger or other device along while reading the words aloud. Spoken words match written words one-to-one. Print is what the reader reads. Readers look at the print from left to right.

- **Analyze the pictures.** After reading the book, go back and explore details in a few pictures. "What is happening in the pictures that makes the story funnier?" Pictures add to the story and sometimes give clues about unknown words. Children who are encouraged to seek out these details are likely to become better readers.

## *26 Letters and 99 Cents*
by Tana Hoban  Scholastic, 1988

- **Front or back?** Notice that the alphabet part of this book starts in one direction and the counting part starts in the opposite direction. Compare the organization of this book to other familiar books. Ask children to figure out what is different. Why do they think Hoban did this? Books have similar parts, but they can be organized in different ways.

- **Recognize upper- and lower-case letters.** Call children's attention to both the capital and lower-case forms of a letter, "This is a capital A… and this is a lower-case a." What do you notice is the same about them? What is different? What words begin with the letter A? (airplane). The same letter can have different shapes. Some words always begin with capital letters, like children's names.

- **Name more.** After reading the book several times, ask children to name some other common objects that begin with the same letters. Focus on these common consonants at first (B, C, D, F, M, N, P, R, S, T). Trace over the letters so children can feel the differences. If possible let children feel and use sandpaper letters, letter tiles, and magnetic letters as well. Letters stand for spoken sounds. Some letters are at the start of LOTS of words.

- **Learn about money.** Set up a pretend grocery store, pet shop, or restaurant. Children write and design signs, price lists or tags, and menus. Use real or imaginary money for customers to use in paying and for clerks to make change. Look at newspaper ads with prices and go "shopping" with a given amount of money. Numerals can be written in words or symbols that mean the same thing. Readers use written numbers in everyday life.

## *Amazing Grace*
by Mary Hoffman  pictures by Caroline Binch  Scholastic, 1991

- **Tell personal stories.** The important message in this book is that people can be successful when they REALLY try and work hard for something. Ask children to talk about some amazing things they have done: how Amber really worked hard and wouldn't quit when she was learning to ride her bicycle; or how proud Ben is now that he knows his telephone number. Share with children something you worked hard to learn or to achieve. Talking with children about important book messages helps them listen, ask good questions, and relate events in books to their own lives.

- **Branch out.** Many good stories are mentioned in this book (Joan of Arc, Anansi the Spider, Helen of Troy, Hiawatha, Mowgli and the Jungle Stories, Aladdin and His Magic Lamp, Peter Pan, Romeo and Juliet). Find books with these stories or tell them with puppets or on a flannel board. Share a story that you remember enjoying when you were young. One good story leads to many others. Everyone has favorite stories that they remember for a long time.

## *I Know an Old Lady*

illustrated by G. Brian Karas                                                               Scholastic, 1980

- **Sing!** This book is an illustrated version of a classic children's song. Talk about how you sang it as a child. Sing it together – with lots of expression. Children want to be like the adults they know and respect. When children know important adults in their lives enjoy reading and talking about books, they will want to become readers, too.

- **Vary the repeats.** The story repeats and builds as it goes along. After a few pages, children enjoy saying the repeat. Ask them to do it differently each time, such as quietly, slowly, fast, singing. Children who are actively engaged in reading stories see themselves as readers who can make meaning of written words.

- **Pick up new words.** Be sure to help children figure out any unfamiliar words (perhaps, absurd). Relate the meanings to familiar things in their lives. When children understand spoken words, they grasp the meaning of the text more fully, and it will be easier for them to learn to read the words.

## *Ben's Trumpet*

by Rachel Isadora                                                                           Scholastic, 1989

- **Explore major themes.** Some children may be eager to talk about times they were teased or how grownups helped them learn to do something. What skills do children want to learn? (tie shoes, write their names). Make a K-W-L chart (what we Know, what we Want to learn, and what we Learned) to record children's progress. Reading can lead to discussion, to asking questions, to writing, and to learning more things.

- **Introduce instruments.** Ask older children to play instruments in the jazz band (piano, saxophone, drums, trumpet, trombone) for younger children. Listen closely to the different sounds that each one makes. Notice how the musicians play each one (ivory keys, metal keys, drum sticks, valves, slide). Match the instruments to their names and pictures in the book. If possible, allow children to try out some instruments for themselves. Books tell about and have pictures of real things. The more hands-on experiences children have with ideas in books, the more meaningful reading will be to them.

*Note: Books are listed alphabetically by the first author's last name.*

**Recommended Books and Learning Experiences**

## Children's Books and Related Early Literacy Activities

- **Explore music.** Look at musical scores of songs children know with someone who sings or plays an instrument. Point out that music uses two symbol systems: words (lyrics) and music (staff, notes, rests). Listen with children to jazz and a variety of other music. Try to pick out the different instrument sounds. Listening for distinctive sound details helps children become more aware of other sounds, including letter sounds, too.

### *Itsy Bitsy Spider*

retold and illustrated by Iza Trapani                                      Scholastic, 1993

- **Sing along.** The first part of this story is the familiar nursery rhyme/action song that children probably already know. Sing or say the rhyme together. Sometimes books start out with things people already know and enjoy.

- **Notice the pictures.** The rest of the book details the further adventures of the spider. Pause and ask open-ended questions to encourage children to explore the beautiful pictures. Look for spiders and their webs. Cut or tear strips of paper to make spiders. How many legs do they have? Pictures add to stories and sometimes help readers figure out new words. Children who notice details will find it easier to learn to read.

- **Finish the rhyme.** The story is told in a rhyme. When reading the book a second time, pause so children can supply the rhyming words: waterspout/out; wall/fall; blow/go; pail/tail; door/more; chair/air; asleep/creep; tree/me; dry/try; stop/top; spun/done/sun. Use these same words to invent new rhymes, too! Being able to hear the similarities in spoken words is important to see how speaking and writing are related. Words that sound alike often, but not always, end in the same letters.

### *Harold's ABC*

by Crockett Johnson                                                        Scholastic, 1999

- **Make wishes.** On every page, Harold sees a letter and turns the letter into something that he wants that begins with that letter. Ask children what they would like that begin with some of the letters. Encourage them to write the letters and draw pictures of their wishes. Many words begin with the same letter. Words can be represented by letters and/or by pictures.

- **Trace letters.** Children take turns tracing the letters (printed in brown) with their fingers and then finding them again on the facing page. In a group, ask children whose names begin with those letters to trace them. Knowing letters of the alphabet is very important for learning to read. Children are most interested in the letters that they see many times, especially the letters in their names.

- **Hunt for new words.** Build vocabularies together. Ask children what some of the words mean – and find out by using a dictionary, looking at the pictures, or asking someone who can explain them (attic, continued, dipper, excursion, edifice, etcetera, elevator, genial, hastened, hobby horse, rocketed, orbiting, planet, parachute, sea serpent, telescope, ermine, trudged). When children understand more words, it is easier for them to grasp the meaning of written or spoken material.

# Chapter 3

## *Over in the Meadow*

illustrated by Ezra Jack Keats  Scholastic, 1971

- **Meet more animals.** This book is a traditional counting rhyme about many common creatures. Some of these farm animals may not be familiar to city children. If at all possible, visit a farm, zoo, or nature center so children can see these creatures first-hand. The beautiful illustrations can also help children recognize the shapes, colors, relative sizes, and names of these animals. Find these same animals in other books, songs, nursery rhymes, puzzles, and puppet figures. Animals (and other story ideas) can be shown in many different ways. The more ways children see the same concept represented, the more likely they are to understand other stories and information.

- **Sing and act out the story.** Children choose an animal in the book and make a simple mask, paper-bag puppet, modeling compound figure, or other representation of the animal. Together, sing the story with the characters each playing their parts. Hands-on, active experiences with ideas and symbols make reading more memorable.

- **Compare rhyming words.** Some of the rhyming words end in the same letters (rime) and others do not. Go on a treasure hunt to find some of each. Talk about the relationships between language sounds and letters. List other rhyming words and figure out whether they end the same or not. In English, sometimes words that have the same sounds also have the same letters; sometimes they do not.

## *The Snowy Day*

by Ezra Jack Keats  Scholastic, 1962

- **What is snow?** This classic story describes Peter's experiences on the day he wakes up to find his world covered in snow. The language is poetic and creates a mood of magic and wonder. It is a book for sharing with children on many days – snowy or not. Ask children what they know about snow. "What is snow made of? In what season does it snow? How is snow made? What shape are snowflakes?" If snow is available, watch it melt indoors (or observe ice cubes as they melt). Reading is a jumping-off point for learning more about science and nature.

- **Dig deeper!** On a deeper level the book addresses adventures, delight in the world of nature, the pleasure that comes from thinking about fun times. What memorable adventures have children had? Draw or paint pictures of these fun times. Display them as a mural. Stories happen to people. People enjoy remembering their own stories in words and pictures.

- **Find snow.** The word snow or a compound word that includes snow can be found on every page. Look for snow on every page! Write snow outdoors in huge letters in sidewalk chalk. Draw the letters in sand with a stick, much like Peter uses his stick. Emerging readers can learn to identify important words.

*Note: Books are listed alphabetically by the first author's last name.*

**Recommended Books and Learning Experiences**

### Children's Books and Related Early Literacy Activities

## *From Acorn to Zoo and Everything in Between in Alphabetical Order*

by Satoshi Kitamura      Scholastic, 1992

- **Catch the questions.** This engaging alphabet book asks a question on each page. The answer to the question is found in the pictures, and the answer starts with the letter featured on the page. After children realize the pattern, ask them to identify the question, the letter, and to predict what they think the answer will be. Authors use many different techniques to present their stories, and to make sure readers enjoy them!

- **Match pictures and letters.** Ask children to name the featured letter and as many of the pictures as they can. Help children give responses that start with the featured letter. For example, if the letter is B and a child points to the small bird and says, "crow," respond by saying, "It could be a crow, but the name has to start with the /b/ sound. What color is it? (Black) Yes, it's black. What bird's name begins with black? (Blackbird)." Being able to hear the similarities in spoken words is important for learning how speaking and writing are related. Words that sound alike often have the same letters.

- **Go beyond the names.** Be sure to name some of the less familiar objects on each page and explain something about them. With apricot, an adult might say, "That's a fruit that is like a little peach." Better yet, let children examine both real fruits to identify the differences. And be sure to eat juicy apricots! Hands-on experiences that engage children's senses are far more memorable than simple explanations.

## *The Wheels on the Bus*

by Maryann Kovalski      Scholastic, 1987

- **Sing along!** A little girl and her grandmother go shopping. While waiting to catch the bus for home, they sing the traditional children's song. Children enjoy singing while reading along. The words are very repetitive and it is easy to see word boundaries. When people read or sing, each word has a corresponding word in print.

- **Get on the bus.** If possible, take a bus ride together. Before boarding, look for the parts of the bus in the song (wheels, wipers). Follow up the experience with pretend play about bus trips. Obtain a large packing box, such as a refrigerator box, from an appliance store. With the children, build a bus. Add more parts than are in the song. Write new song verses to match the bus. Reading can lead to many more adventures related to the story – and beyond!

## *The Carrot Seed*

by Ruth Kraus      pictures by Crockett Johnson      Scholastic, 1945

- **Read with expression.** This story is a great one to read with different voices. Use a higher pitch for mother and a lower pitch for father. Ask children to imitate the voices, too. Play "Who Is It?" by speaking in a voice and asking children to identify the character, in this and other books. Characters in books (and people and animals in real life) speak in different voices. The sounds can be high, low, loud, soft, and have many other characteristics.

- **Be your best.** This story has a lovely message about doing one's best and believing in oneself. Ask children to remember times when they, or someone they know, did their best. How did that person feel? How did their families or friends feel? Use puppets, dolls, or small figures to act out scenarios. Stories are about people's lives. Lots of people share the same experiences.

## *Inch by Inch*

by Leo Lionni                                                                                        Scholastic, 1960

- **Prepare for the story.** Before reading, ask children to talk about the worms they have seen. Use a thumb and forefinger, flattened out and then bunched up, to show children how an inchworm moves. Have children try it, too. "Who knows how long an inch is?" Show an inch on a ruler. Who has seen a worm this small? Background knowledge helps children better understand both fiction and nonfiction stories.

- **Predict the trick.** Introduce the story by explaining that the inchworm is going to play a trick on a bird. Ask open-ended questions to encourage children to think about what might happen: "What kind of trick do you think a worm could play on a bird?" After reading the story, ask "How did the inchworm get away from the nightingale?" When children have a vested interest in the outcome and listen for particulars, they are more attentive as the story unfolds.

- **Identify bird characteristics.** Many different types of birds appear in this story. Ask children to describe and compare each bird's characteristics, such as "The toucan has a big, colorful beak." Compare the birds in the story to other birds children know, from parakeets to pigeons. Children are more observant when they are looking for specific details in illustrations or in the text.

## *Swimmy*

by Leo Lionni                                                                                        Scholastic, 1989

- **What will happen next?** In this classic children's story, a little black fish organizes his friends to solve the story's problem. Use the story structure to ask children to predict what may happen next, to identify the problem and solution, and to talk about the author's deeper message (work together to solve a big problem). Readers use the illustrations, what they know about the situation, and the elements of the story (characters, plot, setting), to anticipate what happens next.

- **Create an ocean.** Lionni introduces many unusual ocean creatures, depicts them in great detail using a variety of art techniques, and uses rich descriptive language to tell the story. Working together, paint the background for a large ocean mural. Use sponges and paper doilies to make sea creature prints in Lionni's style. Cut or tear construction paper fish and glue them to the scene. Retell the story using the mural. Hands-on experiences with new vocabulary and concepts make learning more memorable. Children can demonstrate what they are learning in a variety of concrete, meaningful ways.

*Note: Books are listed alphabetically by the first author's last name.*

**Recommended Books and Learning Experiences**

Children's Books and Related Early Literacy Activities

## *On Market Street*
by Arnold & Anita Lobel　　　　　　　　　　　　　　　　　Scholastic, 1981

- **What else can you buy?** This is an unusual alphabet book. Each letter is the first letter of a word for something one can buy "on Market Street." Ask children to think of other things they might buy. Write the words on cards, and/or find pictures in magazines or catalogs. Sort the words by first letters. Make an alphabet of other items to buy "on Market Street." Children can be book authors and illustrators, too, by extending their knowledge in a familiar format.

- **Find the letter.** Ask children to find the letter at the beginning of each word. Look for the letters in lots of other places. Words are made of letters.

- **Dress yourself!** The illustrations are fun, too. On each page a person appears in an outfit made entirely of the object names. For example, on the page for T, the clothing is made up of toys. On large paper, children trace the outlines of each other's bodies. They then dress themselves in items that begin with the first letters of their names – either by drawing, writing words, and/or finding pictures in recycled magazines. How delightful! Book illustrations can lead to many more creative ways to represent ideas and build on what children already know.

## *At the Laundromat*
by Christine Loomis　　　illustrated by Nancy Poydar　　　Scholastic, 1993

- **Let's do laundry!** Pictures and rhyming phrases tell this story. Before reading, talk with children about their experiences doing laundry at the Laundromat or at home. "Who sorts the clothes? How do they decide? Who puts in the detergent? Where are the clothes dried? How do people fold clean clothes?" If possible, do some hand laundry, such as washing doll clothes, and talk about each step of the process. Stories can describe things that people do every day and tell about things that are familiar.

- **Enjoy the words.** Look at the pictures and ask children to tell what is happening in each one. Then go back and read the rhyming phrases on each page. Have fun saying each of the words and figuring out what they mean (mingle, jiggle, gushes, plumbers, screech, rumble). Show the actions with body movements (jiggle). Some words are fun to say and may even sound or feel like what they mean.

- **What's missing?** After children are familiar with this book, pause so they can add the rhyming word while reading ("Soap spills. Washer _____ (fills."). Rhyming words help children associate letters with sounds. Completing sentences with missing words encourages children to listen carefully and think about sounds and words.

## *At the Library*
by Christine Loomis　　　illustrated by Nancy Poydar　　　Scholastic, 1993

- **Explore libraries.** What a great tie-in with the classroom lending library! Talk with children about their library experiences. "Were there lots of books on the shelves? Did you listen to a story? How were books checked out? Did the librarian use a computer?" Use the book to build enthusiasm about resources in the classroom and community. Talk about what to look for when choosing a book. Review the checkout process. Remind children about how to take good care of books. Talking about familiar, concrete personal experiences helps children gain more from the pictures and text in a book.

- **Read the pictures.** Go through the book just looking at the pictures. Children describe what is happening on each page. Listen for what they understand and have yet to grasp about the workings of a library. Focus on these points when reading the book or in further discussion. Adults can figure out what children are ready to learn by listening to their interpretations of illustrations and stories.

- **Concentrate on the words.** After these activities, go back and read the rhyming phrases on each page. Help children figure out the meanings of any unfamiliar words (galore, gnomes – see the picture in the poster, prowl, peer, tumble, jumble). Children use a variety of different strategies to figure out word meanings, such as context, illustrations, and their own experiences with similar words.

## *Flossie and the Fox*
by Patricia C. McKissack   pictures by Rachel Isadora   Scholastic, 1986

- **Start with basic information.** A girl named Flossie outsmarts a sly fox that tries to steal her eggs. Introduce the story by explaining that foxes eat chickens and eggs, and that dogs chase foxes and will try to kill them. Background information about the context of the story – characters, plot, and setting – helps children better understand its meaning.

- **Build vocabulary.** Help children figure out the meanings of new words (critter, rascal, commenced, curtsy, disgusted, terrified, spring, leaping, confidence, exceedingly, whimper, glance, miserably). Try out the action words (spring, leap, curtsy). Stories make sense when children know what the words mean.

- **Read in different voices.** Flossie speaks in an everyday country dialect. The fox uses smooth and fancy words, and "talks like a book." Read them as authentically as possible. Ask children what they hear different about the two styles of speaking. Try saying things together using the two expressions so children get the feel for various pronunciations and word selections. Different words and speaking styles fit different characters and situations. Spoken language may not be the same as the words used in books.

## *David McPhail's Animals A to Z*
by David McPhail   Scholastic, 1989

- **Which pictures have no words?** Each page has words for some of the objects in the picture that start with the featured letter. Several more objects starting with that letter are found in the pictures. Ask children to find them. (Answers are on the last two pages.) Phonemic awareness is the ability to hear beginning sounds that are the same. It is an important skill for learning to read.

- **Hunt for more sounds.** Search for other objects that start with the same sound. Use alphabet blocks, magnetic letters, or handmade letter signs. Sort the objects by letter. What can be done about letters that have no objects? Solve the problem together. Opportunities for applying phonemic awareness are all around.

*Note: Books are listed alphabetically by the first author's last name.*

**Recommended Books and Learning Experiences**

Children's Books and Related Early Literacy Activities

## *First Flight*

by David McPhail                                                                                          Scholastic, 1987

- **Remember other trips.** Before reading, talk with children about trips or airplane rides they have taken. Listen for what children understand, as well as any gaps in their knowledge about airplane travel. While reading, point out how the little boy's experience was similar to their own adventures, such as buying a ticket and looking out the window. Stories can be about real-life events. Lots of people share similar experiences and enjoy telling their own stories.

- **Notice details in the illustrations.** Ask children to notice what is happening in the pictures. What events are not described with words? The little boy has some very interesting adventures with his friends that aren't talked about in the print. When reading picture books, there is often more information in the pictures that make the story even more fun and interesting.

## *How Do Apples Grow?*

by Betsy Maestro             illustrated by Giulio Maestro                   Scholastic, 1992

- **Snack on apples.** With children, prepare apples in a variety of ways: baked, sliced with chunks of cheese, applesauce, fritters, and any local or ethnic recipes that fit the group. Taste-test several varieties and chart children's favorites. For a curriculum-integrated activity, read recipes, measure ingredients, track cooking time, and record children's thoughts about the finished product. Broadening children's experiences with familiar topics makes books far more meaningful.

- **Study the pictures.** Many pictures in this book are labeled to demonstrate some of the concepts explained in the text. Pause and talk about the pictures. Relate pictures to the text. Illustrations can help readers learn even more about the topic of a book.

- **Visit an orchard.** If possible, visit an orchard at least three times, from early spring when trees are in bloom through fall when apples are harvested. Take notes and pictures to record changes in the trees and their fruit. Seeing the concepts in a book come alive in nature adds greatly to the understanding of the words.

- **Examine apples.** When eating raw apples, look for the parts of the sepal on the end opposite the stem. Slice the apple crossways and find the five little seed compartments. Count how many seeds are in each apple. Make a chart to show children's favorite apple colors (red, green, yellow, speckled). Books help people learn more about everyday experiences.

## *How Kids Grow*

by Jean Marzollo             photographs by Nancy Sheehan              Scholastic, 1998

- **Wonder!** Read the title of the book, and look at the pictures of children on the cover. Ask, "What do you think this book will be about?" Children who are curious about the book are likely to pay more attention while it is being read. Making predictions about a book's contents helps children develop their abilities to interpret pictures and to select books that appeal to them.

- **Who can do it?** While reading the book, pause to ask children if they can do the things that the children on the pages of the book can do. If children know another child who is the same age as the one featured, talk about the things that child is able to do. What a great opportunity to ask families to share baby pictures of children at earlier ages! Books help people learn more about themselves and others. People share lots of common experiences and memories.

- **Record changes.** With children, start a diary or timeline showing how they change over the course of the school year. Record heights, shoe sizes, and skills (tie shoes, recognize first letter of name, count to 5) at the beginning and once a month throughout the year. Share these with families as a farewell gift at the end of the year. Words can be used to document personal information and memories that delight people.

### *I Am Water*

by Jean Marzollo         illustrated by Judith Moffatt         Scholastic, 1996

- **How do we use water?** To introduce this book, ask children to list the ways that they use water every day. Write and illustrate a list. Add to it as children notice more ways. Books help people be more aware of the world and the importance of everyday routines.

- **The words, "I am" are repeated on every page.** Point to the words each time they appear. The next time, children can find the words. Children who are actively engaged in the reading of books see themselves as readers and are more interested in what they read.

- **Water collage.** Search through recycled magazines for pictures of people using water (swim, laundry, cooking, bathe pets). Make a collage of ways to use water. Talk, too, about ways to use less of this precious natural resource. Young children are establishing life-long habits that affect the Earth's ecology. Reading about the topic, and applying what they learn in their lives, helps them learn how to treat the Earth in friendly ways.

### *Farm Alphabet Book*

by Jane Miller         Scholastic, 2000

- **Visit a farm or agricultural display.** Urban and suburban children are likely to have little experience with objects found on farms. If possible, see some of them first-hand before reading the book, so that word definitions will be familiar. Children's reading vocabularies are built from personal experiences with the words in books.

- **Upper or lower?** Miller's book uses both capital and lowercase letters in names of the objects. Ask children to describe the similarities and differences in the two alphabet forms. Trace the shapes. Find the same letters in recycled magazines, on signs, and in other places. Letters come in a variety of shapes and sizes. The more familiar children are with this variety, the better prepared they are to read.

- **Match letters to words and words to pictures.** When reading the book a second time, encourage children to find the word on the page, the word in the definition that begins with the letter that they found, and the picture of the word. Start with letters that are most important to them, such as the first letters of their names. When children see that letters make words, that words name objects, and that objects can be represented in

*Note: Books are listed alphabetically by the first author's last name.*

**Recommended Books and Learning Experiences**

### Children's Books and Related Early Literacy Activities

pictures, they see how symbols are used to express spoken words and ideas. Reading is interpreting symbols!

## *Who Stole the Cookies?*
by Judith Moffat  Scholastic, 1997

- **Chant along!** This is the traditional children's chant accompanied by beautiful collage illustrations. Children who know the chant love to read the story. Spoken words can be written in print. When children know the words, they can read along with an adult and feel confident about their ability to learn to read other text as well.

- **Ask questions.** This chant is based on a question. Play similar word games in which children ask or answer questions to find solutions, such as riddles and guessing games. Talk about how questions are different than statements. Ponder this idea with children: "Why do people ask questions?" Questions are another way people use words to find out more information. Questions often begin with words such as who, what, where, when, or why. Curious, courteous people expect to hear or find answers to their questions.

## *It's a Party*
by Daniel Moreton & Samantha Berger  Scholastic, 1999

- **Point to the party words.** Show children the words as you read. Spoken words match written words one-to-one. Print is what the reader reads.

- **What happens at a party?** Together, talk about what the children are doing on each page. Ask children to share memories of parties they have attended. If possible, make a class party book using photos. Categorize the pictures by type of party: picnic, birthday, surprise, graduation, or new baby, for example. Suggest that children plan a party for their families – and then do it! Books connect children with each other and their families.

## *The Day Jimmy's Boa Ate the Wash*
by Trinka Hakes Noble   pictures by Steven Kellogg   Scholastic, 1980

- **Read with expression.** Change voices when reading the mother's questions and the little girl's answers. Voice expression can help children understand how this story works. On a second reading, let children take the parts, using their own different tones of voice. Voices sound differently when asking a question, and people who ask questions usually expect a response. Successful students ask lots of questions and give lots of thoughtful answers.

- **What's so funny?** Many of the funny parts of this story happen in the pictures. Do children notice them? If so, ask them to explain why they are laughing. If not, point out the picture and wait for them to figure out what's so funny. Prompt children to be observant and recognize those who do pick up on details! Noticing details is essential for learning to read.

Chapter 3

## *Animal Action ABC*

by Karen Pandell　　　wildlife photography by Art Wolfe　　　Scholastic, 1998
child photography by Nancy Sheehan

- **Stress the rhyming words.** Most of the pages of this book have a pair of rhyming words. Read the page with stress on the rhyme. Careful listening helps children identify the relationship of sounds to whole words.

- **Get into the act!** After reading the book, ask children to pick some of the pages to act out what is happening. Confucius said, "I hear and I forget. I see and I remember. I do and I understand."

- **Explore animals.** The last few pages of the book give interesting facts about the animals in the pictures. Each day, children choose an animal to learn more about. Read the page, look at the pictures, find more pictures of the animals in their natural habitats, draw life-size animals with sidewalk chalk, and make animal sounds. Find out the names of animal groups and their babies. Make animal puppets with paper bags so children can represent features such as their eyes, ears, noses, whiskers, necks, fur, and other identifying characteristics. Books are just the beginning of the adventure of learning about almost anything!

## *Families Are Different*

written and illustrated by Nina Pellegrini　　　Scholastic, 1991

- **Appreciate families.** This book explains the concept of adoption, and explores the idea that there are many different types of families, but all families are bound by love. Before or after reading, encourage children to talk about their families. Focus on similarities and connections among the people in their stories. Display pictures of children's families with captions. Suggest that children read the captions to each other or to their families. Books are a great way for people to learn more about each other and appreciate the people we love.

- **While reading, stop along the way and explain concepts they may not understand.** Vocabulary building – when children understand spoken words, it is easier for them to learn to read them.

- **Who is in my family?** After reading, talk with children about their families. "Who are the members? How is your family like the one in the book? How is your family different?" Ask children to draw pictures of their families – they're likely to include pets! Mat the pictures on a slightly larger, contrasting color of paper. Include short, dictated paragraphs describing the picture. Date the art. Families will treasure these forever. Books have meaning to people's lives. The ideas in books can be personalized with words and pictures.

## *And the Cow Said Moo!*

by Mildred Phillips　　　pictures by Sonja Lamut　　　Scholastic, 2001

- **Who says what?** In this book, the cow says the same thing on each page to the different animal that is pictured. "Good morning, ____ (animal). Say Moo! Say Moo! If I say Moo,

*Note:
Books are listed alphabetically by the first author's last name.*

67

**Recommended Books and Learning Experiences**

### Children's Books and Related Early Literacy Activities

why don't you?" After the first couple of pages, pause to encourage children to identify the animal name by looking at the picture. Words and sounds that can be spoken can be written. Pictures can help readers figure out what the words are about.

- **Search for Moo!** The word Moo appears in a special font on each page. It is an important word in this book. Help children find that word. Then they can find it themselves on other pages. Words look the same each time they are printed.

- **Oops!** When rereading the story, intentionally say another animal sound or name. Children enjoy the humor and quickly pick up on the change! Ask children to invent their own stories with different animal sounds. Put the children's words and pictures into a simple book or scroll to read again and again, too. Changing familiar details in a book encourages careful listening and boosts children's imaginative thinking.

## *Apples and Pumpkins*
by Anne Rockwell        pictures by Lizzy Rockwell        Scholastic, 1991

- **Point out new words.** Help children identify unfamiliar things by matching words with the pictures (barn, silo, geese, chicken, baby chicks, turkey, fields, orchard, vines, jack-o-lantern). Children who have larger vocabularies will more easily learn to read and understand the information.

- **From farm to table.** Talk about and find more pictures of how apples, pumpkins, and other fruits and vegetables are grown on farms. Explain that they are taken to the grocery store on airplanes and in trucks. If possible, visit a working farm or farmer's market in different seasons. Watch delivery trucks being unloaded. Go to the grocery store with a shopping list to find the foods described in the book. Plant seeds and watch them grow. Create a mural showing the process of growing foods from farm to children's tables. Farmers are essential because they grow food for every person on Earth. Reading about the basic processes that relate directly to children's lives builds an appreciation for how people are interdependent.

- **Pretend to be farmers.** Provide blocks, miniature vehicles, pretend animals, and other props for children to set up their own farms. Label their farms with words from the book. If possible, grow plants and enjoy the harvest. Ideas in books can be translated into concrete objects and actions.

## *One Duck Stuck*
by Phyllis Root        Scholastic, 1998

- **Invent new counting rhymes.** This is a counting story told in rhyme. The story is filled with words that illustrate this concept: words that sound alike at the ends, usually have the same letters at the ends, too. Ask children to invent similar counting rhymes with different rhyming words. Language sounds and letters are related.

- **What's the point?** The story ends with a creative solution to the duck's problem that implies an important moral. Neither the solution, nor the moral, is clearly stated. Children must "listen between the lines" to find out how the duck gets unstuck. Ask them to describe what they think happened at the end. Sometimes an author wants readers to figure things out for themselves. People use what they already know to figure it out.

## *I Know Why I Brush My Teeth*

by Kate Rowan            illustrated by Katharine McEwen            Scholastic, 2000

- **What do you know?** Read the title and look at the cover together. Ask children why they brush their teeth. Make a list to compare with the text. Reading gives people opportunities to remember what they know and build on that information.

- **Match the list with the book.** While reading the book, pause when something Sam knows is related to the things on the list. If necessary at first, prompt children to see the similarities. Books have meaning to people's lives and to things people do every day.

- **Interpret the pictures.** Some pages have drawings that explain more about what Sam and his mother talk about. Reflect on those that are especially pertinent for children. Pictures can contain more information. Look at them carefully for details not found in the words.

- **Brush up!** If possible, borrow impressions of a human mouth and/or a poster with teeth from a dentist. Demonstrate how to brush teeth. When children brush their teeth, remind them to brush their incisors, canines, or molars. Healthy habits can be developed many ways, including by reading.

## *The Three Little Pigs: An English Folktale*

retold by Jeanette Sanderson            Rigby, 2003

- **Gather a group.** This version of the childhood classic has large print that ensures that a single child, a small group, or a larger gathering will be able to see the print details. Vary the ways in which stories are shared with children. Stories can be enjoyed one-on-one, in small groups, or with lots of friends.

- **Repeat the refrains.** After reading the story one time, children enjoy repeating the famous refrains, "Not by the hair of my chinny-chin-chin," and "Then I'll huff and I'll puff and I'll blow your house in." Children who are actively engaged in reading are more likely to be attentive and to follow the action.

- **What is similar?** As written here, huff, puff, and blow are written in a larger font. Ask children to compare the three words. "What is the same? What is different?" If necessary, point out that huff and puff sound alike, and look alike, at the end. Letters and sounds have important relationships.

## *Butterfly Alphabet*

by Kjell B. Sandved            Scholastic, 1996

- **Look closely!** Sandved traveled all over the world taking photos of butterflies and moths. He found the letters of the alphabet in the beautiful patterns in the butterflies' wings. On one page, the part of the pattern that has the letter is shown. On the facing page, the photo of the whole butterfly can be seen. With children, look carefully to find the letters, first in the detail and then on the whole butterfly. Distinguishing letters from distracting colors and designs takes a keen eye, much like reading!

- **Trace the letters.** Encourage children to use their fingers to trace the letter on the page with text and to find the letter in the photograph. Then draw the same letters in the air.

*Note: Books are listed alphabetically by the first author's last name.*

### Children's Books and Related Early Literacy Activities

**Recommended Books and Learning Experiences**

Form the letters using your bodies. Look for them all around. Letters of the alphabet can appear in a variety of forms. They are still the same letter.

- **Letters to words to sentences.** Each page has a sentence about butterflies that includes a word that begins with the featured letter. Encourage children to name the letter. Think of new words that begin with the same letter and use them to start new sentences. Letters are put together to make words and words form sentences – an essential understanding for learning to read.

- **Get to know butterflies.** At the end of the book are several pages of information about moths and butterflies. Pick out the information that is of most interest to children. Visit a butterfly display or ask someone in the community to show the group some colorful specimens. Which butterflies and moths live in your area? Find out about butterfly and moth life cycles. Make replicas of each stage with modeling compounds. Label each stage with words. Books are sources of information and can lead to more questions and interesting discoveries about fascinating things.

## *Down on the Farm*
written by Greg Scelsa    illustrated by Susan Drawbaugh    Creative Teaching Press, 1994

- **Who are they and what sounds do they make?** Many beginning reading books and related learning experiences assume that children can identify common farm animals. After reading the book, make up memory games. Point to an animal and ask children to say its name. What sound does it make? Then turn the tables and give the name of an animal (or the sound it makes). Children find the animal's picture in the book. Playing games with words make literacy activities doubly enjoyable!

- **Sing along.** After reading the book one time, children enjoy singing it. For those adults who don't read music, make up a tune or ask a musician to help everyone learn the music. Compare music to letters and words. How are they similar? Different? Music is another symbol system, very much like words. The two are combined every time people sing!

- **Word search!** After children are familiar with this book, ask them to help find some of the words (cow, pig, dog) on the facing pages. Find the same words in other books, on posters, and in magazines. Recognizing whole words is an important early literacy skill.

## *Where the Wild Things Are*
by Maurice Sendak                                                                Scholastic, 1991

- **Dig deep!** On the surface, this book is a tale of a rebellious little boy who has an exciting adventure in a far-away land filled with monsters. The story works on many deeper levels, as well. With children, consider open-ended questions like these: "Do you think Max has a real adventure or is it all a dream? Could this story really happen? How do you know? How do you feel when you get in trouble? What scares you the most? When you get afraid, what do you do?" Authors and illustrators often have messages that make people think. Stories have personal meanings that may be different for each reader.

- **Go wild!** Many children enjoy gnashing their terrible teeth, showing their terrible claws, and roaring their terrible roars along with the story. Why not produce the story as a play? Use stuffed animals to reenact some scenes. For a more elaborate, engaging experience, children decorate simple masks for their chosen character(s) with paper plates and craft sticks. Make costumes with paper grocery bags. Paint rolled paper or use recycled boxes for simple stage sets. Reenact every page in dramatic fashion. Books can come alive by acting out the story with props. Books can get people excited, and then help them calm down.

- **Use caution.** Some children find this book frightening. Read it only when you are confident that children will appreciate it. Point out how the monsters are smiling. Sometimes, just introducing a scary book with a statement such as this can help children deal with the strong emotions: "This book is all about pretending. It couldn't really happen. But it's fun to imagine and dream." Books can bring out all kinds of emotions, so adults choose them with care for children.

### *Brothers and Sisters*

by Ellen B. Senisi                                                                                           Scholastic, 1993

- **Brothers are… Sisters are…** Before reading the book, find out what children know about brothers and sisters. Ask them to complete the sentences about brothers and sisters. Write their responses on a chart. What similarities are there? What differences? What insights can adults gain from listening to children's perceptions about other people? When children reflect on their own experiences, they can then absorb more meaning from a book on the topic.

- **Easy and hard.** Ask children to think about what is the best part about having a brother or sister. Then ask what is the hardest thing about having a brother or sister. Children can learn new vocabulary words and concepts from each other as they discuss concepts from books they read.

### *Chato's Kitchen*

by Gary Soto             illustrated by Susan Guevara              Scholastic, 1995

- **What next?** Chato, the cat, tries to trick his new neighbors into becoming his dinner, but the mice play a trick on him. While reading, stop frequently to ask, "What do you think will happen next? Let's find out!" Making predictions and checking to see if they turn out is an excellent way to help children pay attention to longer stories.

- **Teach each other.** This story uses many words in Spanish and gives English definitions on the back of the title page. English-speaking children enjoy learning these words, and the children who speak Spanish enjoy teaching them to their friends. After children's vocabularies have expanded, show the pictures and ask children to name items in both English and Spanish. Delight in learning new words can be contagious. Children can learn new words from each other.

*Note: Books are listed alphabetically by the first author's last name.*

**Recommended Books and Learning Experiences**

Children's Books and Related Early Literacy Activities

## Dinosaur Roar!

by Paul & Henrietta Strickland                                      Scholastic, 1995

- **Get the opposites!** Most of the dinosaur actions or descriptions in this book are opposites (roar/squeak; fierce/meek; fast/slow). First, read the book for pure enjoyment. The second time, bring up the idea of opposites. Who can name some words that mean something exactly different? Start with familiar words (yes/no; quiet/loud). Together, try to figure out what some of the new words mean, maybe because they are paired with familiar words that are their opposites. The context in which words are used often is helpful in figuring out what they mean.

- **Page to page.** The last word on every other page rhymes. After hearing this book read one time, children enjoy providing the rhyming word on the next page. Hearing sounds at the ends of words is an important reading skill. Completing sentences challenges children to think about meaning more broadly.

## I Love You, Little One

by Nancy Tafuri                                                     Scholastic, 1998

- **How do I love you?** In beautiful, poetic language Tafuri shares many ways that mother animals show love for their young. Before reading the story, ask children to share their ideas about how they show love to people – and how people show their love to them. Write lists and compare the two. What things are similar? What are different? Stories can help people understand themselves, and others, much better.

- **Love new words!** While reading along, explain words in context and by referring to the illustrations (riverbank, mossy, calm, beneath, burrow, meadow, rye, harm, cave, tree hollow). Meanings of words often can be figured out from the story in which they are told, experiences with similar words, and the pictures on the page.

- **Repeat the phrase.** Every page ends with the phrase, "I love you as the _____ loves you, forever and ever and always." After the first few pages, children enjoy saying this phrase. Children who take an active role in storytelling see themselves as readers and listen more carefully to the book sharing.

- **Care for pets.** Explore how pet owners show love for their pets. Visit a pet store, veterinarian's office, or other facility. Read more books about caring for pets. If possible, adopt a suitable animal. Caring for animals – and observing their behaviors – are growth experiences for all involved. Books are sources of information and can lead to exciting new experiences with people and animals.

## Cookie's Week

by Cindy Ward            illustrated by Tomi DePaola               Scholastic, 1990

- **Find familiar words.** On every day of the week, Cookie causes a problem – "everywhere." After reading the book one time, go back and re-read. Pause, and let children read the "everywhere" or "Cookie." Encourage children to insert words and phrases that appear often in a story. Important early reading skills include identifying patterns in storytelling and recognizing sight words that appear often.

- **Explore the calendar.** While reading, encourage children to state the names of the days of the week. Collect various types of calendars. Use them to keep track of daily activities. Make plans and record them on the calendar. Reading is useful in everyday life. Words can help people organize their time.

## A-Counting We Will Go

adapted by Rozanne Lanczak Williams  Creative Teaching Press, 1995
illustrated by Mazry Thelen

- **Count one by one!** Use pennies, stones, or other small objects to place on top of the bugs, frogs, cats, foxes, hens, goats, and bears while counting them. Count blocks on the shelves, napkins on the table, and anything else at hand. Counting involves one-to-one matching as well as memorizing the counting words in sequence. Reading involves one-to-one matching of words in print to words spoken.

- **Stress the rhyming words.** Each set of objects to count uses a pair of rhyming words (bugs/rugs, frogs/logs, cats/mats, foxes/boxes, hens/pens, bees/trees, goats/boats, bears/chairs). When reading the book the first time, stress the words that rhyme. When rereading, leave the second word in the pair blank so children can add it. For example: "We'll count the bugs And put them on _____ (rugs)…" Hearing similar sounds (rhymes) helps children look for similar letters in those words. English words that sound alike often end alike.

## All Through the Week With Cat and Dog

by Rozanne Lanczak Williams  Creative Teaching Press, 1994
illustrated by Catherine Leary

- **Read between the lines.** Ask children why Cat felt "great" on Sunday afternoon. Could it be because she got some exercise? Or maybe because she ate healthy food instead of just sweets and snacks? Stories sometimes lead readers to think about why things happen – they may not always explain everything.

- **Look for patterns.** This book uses many patterns to tell the story. After reading the story the first time, children enjoy participating by repeating one of the patterns, such as days of the week or morning/afternoon on facing pages. Parts of stories may be predictable because of something readers already know.

- **What food?** The pictures on each page clearly illustrate which food is eaten. Read the story, leaving that word blank. "On Monday morning, Dog made _____.)" and ask children to fill in the word. Point to the words to confirm the children's predictions. Words that can be spoken can be written and illustrated.

*Note: Books are listed alphabetically by the first author's last name.*

## Children's Books and Related Early Literacy Activities

**Recommended Books and Learning Experiences**

### *The Bear Went Over the Mountain*

adapted by Rozanne Lanczak Williams  Creative Teaching Press, 1994
illustrated by Anne Kennedy

- **Sing and be silly!** Do you remember the tune to this silly song? If not, just make one up. Reading is fun. Words that can be read can also be sung to music.

- **Read along.** The story uses much repetition. After reading the story and learning the song, children enjoy reading along the second time. Singing is an excellent way to memorize the words to a story or poem.

- **Add lyrics.** Make up some new verses about places in the neighborhood: "The bear went behind the grocery store…." With children, write and illustrate a book about where the bear went in the neighborhood. Stories can be adapted to fit people's lives and familiar places. Words that are spoken and sung can be written and illustrated. English print is written and read from left to right.

### *Bugs Go Marching*

adapted by Rozanne Lanczak Williams  Creative Teaching Press, 1995
illustrated by Jennifer Beck Harris

- **Sing together.** This book is an adaptation of the song "The Ants Go Marching." The text is very repetitious. Sing the story together. Sometimes books look at familiar things in new ways. Words that are spoken can also be sung and illustrated in pictures.

- **Find number words.** The number words are in bold type. While counting the bugs on each page, point out the number words. Then find number words and numerals on familiar things such as paper money, newspaper ads, and written directions. Children can learn to recognize a few important and useful words and their symbols. Knowing a few basic words helps children learn other words.

- **Follow up!** Inside the back cover of the book are several activities for using the book to help children learn more about numbers. Use these ideas, or adapt them, to add to children's understanding of basic math concepts. Books give people new ideas and activities to explore.

### *Buttons, Buttons*

by Rozanne Lanczak Williams  Creative Teaching Press, 1994
photography by Keith Bergher

- **Point to print.** Use a finger or bookmark to point to the words while reading. Spoken words match written words one-to-one. Print is what the reader reads. Readers look at English print from left to right and top to bottom.

- **Read new words.** The word buttons appears predictably many times on each page. Show children how to find it, call out each of the letters, trace around these letters, and form the word button with block or magnet letters. Soon, children will be able to read the word. Children can learn to recognize a few important and useful words. Knowing a few words helps them learn other words.

- **Buttons up!** Find recycled clothing with buttons for children to use during pretend play – and to practice their fine-motor buttoning skills. Collect recycled buttons with which to make collages, add to sculptures, and use in various other art projects. Books can be the source of lots of other activities on the same topic.

## *Cat and Dog*

written by Rozanne Lanczak Williams  Creative Teaching Press, 1994
illustrated by Catherine Leary

- **Follow the leader.** Use a finger or bookmark to point to words while reading. By the end of the book, children may call them out on their own. Spoken words match written words one-to-one. Print is what the reader reads. Readers look at English print from left to right.

- **Copy dog, copy cat.** On the facing pages of this book, the text is almost the same. The dog copies every thing the cat does. After reading the story one time, reread so children can read the second page in each pair. Then play copy cat – a leader says or does something, and everyone else is a copy cat. Be silly and enjoy the game! Readers often use something they already know to figure out what happens next. Reading can lead to more fun!

## *Families Share*

by Rozanne Lanczak Williams  Creative Teaching Press, 1996
photographed by Michael Jarrett

- **What we share.** Before reading the book, ask children to list the things that they share at home. Write the words where all can see. While reading, point out things on the list that are in the book: put away the groceries, play games together, eat together, go to the park. Make new pages to illustrate activities on the children's lists that do not appear in the book. Stories can mirror things that happen in people's lives. They help people understand the similarities in their lives and build connections among them.

- **Rhyme along.** When rereading the book, pause and ask children to provide the rhyming words (play/day; fun/done). Invent new rhyming words to fit the story, too. Many words end with the same sound and the same letters – but not always. Spoken words can also be written. Readers can add their own ideas to fit with the book patterns.

## *The Four Seasons*

by Rozanne Lanczak Williams  Creative Teaching Press, 1994
illustrated by Adjoa Burrowes

- **Explore the seasons.** Find out what children know about the four seasons. "What are the season's names? What season is it now? What season is next? How do we know the season is changing?" Make a chart with children showing signs of the seasons and what children do in each season. Books build on knowledge people already have. Sometimes books help people think about things in new and different ways.

- **Listen to "The Four Seasons."** Play parts of recordings of Vivaldi's "The Four Seasons." Make up words to the songs or play rhythm instruments with them. Dance or paint

*Note: Books are listed alphabetically by the first author's last name.*

**Recommended Books and Learning Experiences**

## Children's Books and Related Early Literacy Activities

along with the music. Look closely at fine art depicting each of the seasons, such as *How Artists See the Weather: Sun, Wind, Snow, Rain* by Colleen Carroll. Ideas in words can also be expressed in music and the visual arts.

- **Celebrate the season!** Devote a week or more to a project that explores a variety of aspects of the current season. Make and record daily weather observations, prepare seasonal dishes, sketch or photograph how plants look, choose appropriate clothing, and become well-versed in what it means to people when it is spring, summer, fall, or winter. People use words to describe things they know, record what they observe, and express their ideas.

---

### *How Many?*

by Rozanne Lanczak Williams  Creative Teaching Press, 1994
illustrated by Diane Valko

- **Follow along.** While reading, use a finger or bookmark to point to the words. When reading the second time, ask children to find some of the familiar or repeated words. Spoken words match written words one-to-one. Print is what the reader reads. Readers of English look at the print from left to right.

- **Point out punctuation!** On the first few pages, the author asks how many legs each animal has. Point out the question mark. What do children think it means? Question marks tell the reader that the author is asking a question – and to read it accordingly. Look for other punctuation, too, such as commas and exclamation points. What do readers do when they see them? Punctuation marks are symbols with meaning. Punctuation helps readers know when to pause and what expression to use to read the words.

- **How many legs?** On the last pages, the author answers the questions. Count the legs and point out the number words (eight, six, four) in the text. With children create a chart to show animals that have two, four, six, eight (or more!) legs. Find or draw pictures of them to make a wall-size mural. Books often help encourage people to do more research, keep track of what they find, and share the information with other people.

- **Match number words and numerals.** Find words and numerals in other places, too, such as price tags, calendars, and telephone numbers. Say the words for the symbols. Numerals can be expressed in words and symbols. Numerals are shortcuts that sometimes make it easier to figure out the meaning.

---

### *How to Make a Mudpie*

by Rozanne Lanczak Williams  Creative Teaching Press, 1994
Photographs by Keith Bergher

- **One by one.** Point to the words while reading, moving a hand along under the sentences. Show where the text on each new page begins. Spoken words match written words one-to-one. Print is what the reader reads. Readers of English look at the print from left to right and top to bottom.

- **Wait a second!** When rereading the book, pause before saying the last word on each page (dirt, water, spoons, pans, stones, leaves, kids, soap) so children can fill in the word.

If they hesitate, ask them to check the picture. Show children the first letter of the word and ask, "Could that word be _____ (the words the children say)? Does (that word) begin with (that letter)?" When readers come to a word they don't know, they think about what makes sense and check the letters in the word to figure it out.

- **Follow recipes.** Use simple recipes to make fruit salad or applesauce, for example. Invent recipes using favorite ingredients – or silly ones like mud pies! People use words to follow directions, make shopping lists, and do other useful tasks.
- **Make mudpies.** Use sand, modeling compounds, or even dirt to make mudpies. Add sticks, grass, and other natural items for a realistic look. Wash hands well after this activity! Books are a source of creative inspiration and fun!

## *I Can Read*

by Rozanne Lanczak Williams                                                                  Creative Teaching Press, 1994
photography by Keith Bergher

- **Follow the leader.** Point to the words, phrases, and sentences while reading. Spoken words match written words one-to-one. Print is what the reader reads. Readers of English look at the print from left to right and top to bottom.
- **Fill it in!** When reading the book again, pause before reading the last word on each page. Children fill it in. If they are unsure, what can they do? (check the picture) If the word they say doesn't match, show them the first letter of the word. "Here's a clue: the first letter of the word is…" When readers come to a word they don't know, they think about what makes sense. They check the letters in the word to try to figure it out.
- **Read along!** Many of the words are repeated on each page, so children soon may be able to read the book themselves, either from memory or by recognizing some of the primary words and filling in the rest. Children feel like successful readers when they recall the words on each page.

## *I See Colors*

by Rozanne Lanczak Williams                                                                  Creative Teaching Press, 1994
photography by Keith Bergher

- **What color?** Pause so children can say the color words. Show that word to the children. Find items all around that are that color – clothing, walls, or toys. Children who learn to recognize a few important and useful words delight in using them and in learning more words.
- **Read along.** The text is very simple and repeats the words "I see" on each page. After hearing it a few times, children may be able to read this book independently or to someone else. Reading is an important skill that is fun to share with others.
- **Word search!** Find the familiar color words on crayons, markers, puzzles, and in context all around them. Learn the color names in the languages spoken by children in the group (red/rojo/rouge/rot). Written and spoken words are ways people communicate. Color words are used to label items. Some words are similar in languages, some are different.

*Note: Books are listed alphabetically by the first author's last name.*

**Recommended Books and Learning Experiences**

Children's Books and Related Early Literacy Activities

## *If a Tree Could Talk*

by Rozanne Lanczak Williams  Creative Teaching Press, 1994
illustrated by Mary Thelen

- **Focus on key words.** Point to a few words that are most familiar to children when reading. Ask them to describe what the word means. Encourage children to call out the letters in the word. Say the sounds of each letter, then put them together in the whole word. Readers have lots of ways of looking at, sounding out, and figuring out the meanings of words.

- **Say it again!** When rereading the book, encourage your children to join in on the repetitions. Invent other phrases that would work equally well. Read the book with the substitute phrases. Challenge children's memories by introducing surprise variations! Some books are written with patterns that soon become familiar. Readers can use their imaginations to adapt books and make them fun for repeated readings.

- **Imagine a tree could talk!** Choose a nearby tree to adopt. Identify what kind of tree it is. Measure its height and girth. Count the number of branches. Trace and make crayon rubbings with its leaves. Sketch and photograph it. Try to figure out how old it is. Watch it change through the seasons. Write a book about how that tree talks to the people who listen to it! Messages come in various forms, including written and spoken words. People find out more information about something in a variety of ways. Ideas in people's imaginations can be expressed in both words and images.

## *It's Melting!*

by Rozanne Lanczak Williams  Creative Teaching Press, 1994
illustrated by Randy Chewning

- **Where's the main word?** The words melt or melts are repeated on each page. Find the word on the cover. Look for it on every page. What letters spell melt? Spell melt with magnetic, felt, or sandpaper letters. Write melt in sand with a stick. Participating with an adult in "reading" gives children confidence that they can become readers, too.

- **What's melting?** After reading this book, thoroughly explore the scientific concept of melting. How long does it take an ice cube to melt (add food coloring to make it easier to see)? Observe melting ice cubes (in various places such as sunshine, refrigerator, indoors). Record how the cubes change as they melt. Keep track of the time it takes. What does the ice change into? Make replicas of the melting cubes at various stages with modeling compound. People discover interesting new things from books and their explorations after reading them.

- **What else is melting?** Find out about how climate change affects glaciers, polar bears, icebergs, growing food, snow-capped mountains, and the water people drink. What difference do these changes in the Earth's climate make to people? What can people do to reduce global warming? Reading alerts people to important messages about things that affect them every day.

## *A Chair for My Mother*

by Vera B. Williams                                                                 Scholastic, 1982

- **What is the real message?** On the surface this heartwarming story is about a family that saves money to buy a comfortable chair after losing its possessions in a fire. On a deeper level it is about how family members love and support one another when facing challenges. After reading the book, ask children to think about what the author's message is. "What is she saying about families? About grandparents? About working hard? About saving money?" Good stories always have a problem for the characters to solve. Authors use many different ways to tell their stories and have their characters solve problems.

- **Warm or cool?** Look through the illustrations. Notice how cool (blue, green) and warm (red, yellow) colors are used in borders to frame the pictures and emphasize important parts of the pictures. Experiment with painting using warm and cool colors side by side. The illustrations in a book can emphasize the message.

- **What are generations?** This book is about three generations of strong, self-reliant women living in the same household. Talk with children about these kinds of questions: "What is a family? What are generations?" When possible, identify the generations in children's families.

## *Bunny Cakes*

by Rosemary Wells                                                                 Scholastic, 1997

- **Predict the word.** In this story, the little bunny, Max, learns much about how people use writing. On many pages, readers can see where his sister wrote a word on the grocery list. Ask children to predict the word added to the grocery list by thinking about the story and checking the pictures. Pictures and words work together to give messages to readers. People use something they already know to figure out how to read new words.

- **Write notes, make lists.** The little bunny, Max, tries to write his own note. Set up a writing center with paper, markers, a children's picture dictionary, and other print materials (telephone book, class roster, magazines). Encourage children to write notes to each other and their families. Make list of things needed for class projects at every opportunity. Encourage invented spellings and the use of illustrations to focus on the message to be conveyed. Writing is directly related to reading. People use letters to make words and put the words in order to make sentences that can be interpreted by another reader.

## *Noisy Nora*

by Rosemary Wells                                                                 Scholastic, 1973

- **Be patient!** Nora is acting out. Her sibling mice are getting all the parent attention. This story is an excellent one for helping children make personal connections to the books they read. Before reading, ask, "Who has ever had to be patient and wait while your parents take care of a brother or sister? How did that make you feel?" Use these understandings of children's perceptions to draw parallels with children's experiences and to point out relevant messages in the book. Books can help people think about how they feel and see things from another person's perspective.

*Note: Books are listed alphabetically by the first author's last name.*

**Recommended Books and Learning Experiences**

## Children's Books and Related Early Literacy Activities

- **How to get attention?** After reading, talk about other ways that Nora could have tried to get her parents' attention. Make a list of possible solutions. Act some of them out to see what might happen. Stories can help people figure out solutions to everyday problems and how to treat each other in real life.

- **Pick out the pieces.** In this story, all the story elements are very clear (characters, setting, problem, resolution, moral/deeper meaning). With each new reading, ask children to focus on one element. For example, "What was the problem Nora had? How was it solved?" Suggest that children represent that story element in drawings, sculpture, pretend play, role play, with puppets, or in some other concrete way. Pull all of the pieces together to review how they fit into a whole story. Stories have common elements. When readers know the elements and how they work together, they can think more deeply about the message and make logical predictions about the stories.

### Read to Your Bunny

by Rosemary Wells                                                Scholastic, 1997

- **Where to read?** On every page, adult and child bunnies are reading and enjoying books together in many different locations. Ask children to describe places where they like to hear stories (on the sofa, at bedtime, on the bus). What are some other places they could try listening to books and stories (under a shady tree, at the doctor's office). Books can be enjoyed almost anywhere!

- **Read to others.** On the last page the child bunny reads to the parent. To whom could children read their favorite stories? Their dolls? Pets? Grandparents? Stuffed animals? How does it make people feel when someone reads to them? Reading the pictures and telling a story from memory, as well as calling out the words, are all-important early reading skills. Sharing books is a time to connect with other people.

### Silly Sally

by Audrey Wood                                                  Scholastic, 1995

- **Look at the end.** Children love wonderfully wacky Silly Sally. She does everything upside down and backwards – and the story rhymes, too! All the rhymes, except one, have the same letters (rime), so this is a good book to use to introduce how words that sound the same at the end often look the same (have the same letter) at the end. Analyzing letters and sounds helps children identify new and related words.

- **Invent more silly stories.** Provide a few simple props such as huge sunglasses, an oversize hat, and a feathery boa. Or choose a few stuffed animals as the primary characters for pretend play. Suggest that children write their own silly stories, either as a group or individually by writing or recording their own ridiculous, imaginative ideas. How does the story begin? What problem does the character need to solve? Where does it take place? How is the problem resolved? Stories all are built around the same parts. People use their imaginations to invent new stories.

*The Little Mouse, The Red Ripe Strawberry, and the Big Hungry Bear*
by Don and Audrey Wood                                        Scholastic, 1994

- **What's the twist?** This funny story has a little twist that may need to be explained to children before reading. The tale is told by a narrator who is talking to the character (mouse) in the pictures. The narrator convinces the little mouse that he has a problem, but the narrator is playing a trick to get something he wants. Authors use many different ways to tell their stories and solve the problems characters have.

- **Act out the story.** Make puppets with paper bags, craft sticks and paper plates, or other handy art materials. Puppets act out the story while characters read the parts. Or encourage children to create simple costumes for the same purpose. Characters can be represented in real life by people or puppets. Stories can be retold in many different ways.

---

## *Seven Blind Mice*
by Ed Young                                                   Scholastic, 1993

- **Enhance understanding.** This story is a variation of the familiar folktale, "Seven Blind Men and the Elephant." Young children may need some introduction to the concept of blindness in order to understand it. One way to do this is to have one child at a time wear a blindfold, reach into a bag or pillowcase, and try to identify a familiar object just by feeling it. Personal, hands-on experiences are essential for children to make sense out of stories that deal with unfamiliar topics.

- **Talk about vision impairments.** Children are likely to have questions about what it means to be blind. Answer them clearly and respectfully. Find out about ways blind people compensate for their lack of vision, such as by using seeing-eye dogs, white canes, developing a keen sense of hearing and touch, and reading Braille. If possible, ask someone who is blind to talk with the children and demonstrate the skills they use in everyday life. Through books and related learning experiences, children gain broadened understandings about themselves and others.

- **What will happen?** This book sets up a wonderful opportunity to make a prediction (What was the strange something by the pond?). Read the rest of the story to see if the predictions are correct. Prediction is one tool readers use to understand books and stories. They think about what might happen, and pay attention to the story to see if the prediction is accurate.

*Note: Books are listed alphabetically by the first author's last name.*

## Appendix A

### Additional Readings

Bowman, B. (Ed.). (2002). *Love to read: Essays in developing and enhancing early literacy skills of African American children*. Washington, DC: National Black Child Development Institute.

Campbell, R. (2001). *Read-alouds with young children*. Newark, DE: International Reading Association.

Codell, E.R. (2003). *How to get your child to love reading: For ravenous and reluctant readers alike*. Chapel Hill, NC: Algonquin Books.

Cullinan, B. (2000). *Read to me: Raising kids who love to read*. New York: Scholastic.

Dupree, H., & Iversen, S. (1996). *Early literacy in the classroom*. Bothell WA: The Wright Group.

Fox, M. (2001). *Reading magic: Why reading aloud to our children will change their lives forever*. San Diego, CA: Harcourt.

Jordano, K. (1996). *Home and back with books*. Cypress, CA: Creative Teaching Press.

National Research Council. (1999). *Starting out right: A guide to promoting children's reading success*. Washington, DC: Author.

New York Times. (2000). *New York Times parent's guide to the best books for children*. New York: Three Rivers Press.

Opitz, M.F. (2000). *Rhymes & reasons*. Portsmouth, NH: Heinemann.

Rog, L.J. (2001). *Early literacy instruction in kindergarten*. Newark, DE: International Reading Association.

Schickedanz, J.A. (1990). *Much more than the ABCs: The early stages of reading and writing*. Washington, DC: National Association for the Education of Young Children.

Trelease, J. (2005). *The read-aloud handbook* (6th ed.). New York: Penguin.

U.S. Department of Education. (1993). *Helping your child learn to read*. Washington, DC: Author.

## Appendix B

### Resources for Educating the Community, Families, and Teachers

• **Community Education Resources**

**Between the Lions Designated Reader Public Awareness Campaign**
Promotes the importance of reading aloud daily.
http://pbskids.org/lions/designated

**First Books**
National nonprofit organization that provides new books to children from low-income families.
1319 F Street, NW, Suite 1000
Washington, DC 20004-1155
866-READ-NOW
202-393-1222
Fax: 202-628-1258
www.firstbook.org

**Jumpstart**
AmeriCorps group that focuses on building literacy and school readiness skills through one-on-one relationships with at-risk preschoolers.
www.jstart.org

**KEEP Books**
Ohio State University produces these small, very inexpensive black-line books for children learning to read. An excellent source for schools and local organizations to provide children with a whole library of books to KEEP at home.

# Appendix

807 Kinnear Road
Columbus, OH 43212
800-678-6484
614-292-2869
www.keepbooks.org

**Literacy, Inc. (LINC)**
Organization's mission is linking community resources to ensure that young readers are good readers.
307 Seventh Avenue
Suite 1603
New York, NY 10001
212-620-5462
Fax: 212-620-0790
http://www.lincnyc.org/

**Reach Out and Read**
Nurses and pediatricians work with parents of birth to 5-year-old children to stress the importance of reading aloud and to give books to children at pediatric check-ups.
Reach Out and Read National Center
56 Roland Street
Suite 100D
Boston, MA 02129-1243
617-455-0600
Fax: 617-455-0601
www.reachoutandread.org

**Reading Is Fundamental**
Organization delivers free books and literacy resources to children and families who need them most. RIF is the nation's oldest nonprofit children's literacy organization.
Reading Is Fundamental, Inc.
1825 Connecticut Avenue, N.W.
Suite 400
Washington, DC 20009
877-RIF-READ
202-536-3400
www.rif.org

• **Resources for Working With Families**

**Even Start**
Federally funded program with four basic components: (1) early childhood education, (2) adult literacy (adult basic and secondary-level education and/or instruction for English language learners), (3) parenting education, and (4) interactive literacy activities for parents and their children. Funding is granted to state education agencies. State agencies then grant funds to local school systems via a formalized process.

U.S. Department of Education
Office of Elementary and Secondary Education
Student Achievement and School Accountability Programs
400 Maryland Avenue, S.W.
Washington, DC 20202
202-260-0826 – Fax: 202-260-7764
e-mail: OESE@ed.gov
www.ed.gov/programs/evenstartformula/index.html

**Motheread, Inc.**
Encourages parents to be reading role models for their children. Designed to empower the family through teaching literacy skills and child development.
3924 Browning Place – Suite 7
Raleigh, NC 27609
919-781-2088 – Fax: 919-571-8579
www.motheread.org

**Parents as Teachers National Center, Inc.**
Provides parents with knowledge and support in the areas of parenting and child development from pregnancy through kindergarten entry.
Attn: Public Information Specialist
2228 Ball Drive
St. Louis, MO 63146
314-432-4330
866-PAT4YOU (866-728-4968)

Fax: 314-432-8963
www.parentsasteachers.org

• **Teacher Education Resources**

**Children's Literacy Initiative**
Provides professional development for teachers of prekindergarten through third grade students in the most effective literacy practices.
2314 Market Street
Philadelphia, PA 19103
215-561-4676
http://cliontheweb.org/

**HeadsUp!**
The National Head Start Association operates **HeadsUp**. The mission is to deliver monthly literacy training via satellite television to Head Start and child care teachers.
National Head Start Association
1651 Prince Street
Alexandria, VA 22314
703-739-0875
Fax: 703-739-0878
http://www.heads-up.org

**Reading a-z.com**
Reading a-z.com offers standards based downloadable literacy resources for teachers.
Learning Page
1840 E. River Road, Suite #320
Tucson, AZ 85718-5834
866-889-3729
Fax: 520-327-9934
Email: razsupport@readinga-z.com
http://www.readinga-z.com

## Appendix C

### Resources to Organize a Lending Library

**Sample Proposal for Funding**
Every funding organization has a unique process through which programs may apply for grants to fund a lending library or any other proposal. Before submitting a request, carefully research possible local, regional, state, and national sources. Choose the funder that best suits a project's purposes and that is likely to be interested in the initiative. This is one example of a proposal. (Donors Choose is a non-profit conduit to connect teachers and funders. Teachers submit project proposals for materials or experiences their students need to learn. Citizen Philanthropists, any person or group viewing the site, choose projects to fund.)
Reading starts at home take home backpacks. (n.d.). Retrieved, August 4, 2006, from
http://www.donorschoose.org/donors

**Reading Starts At Home Take-Home Backpacks**

Subject: **Literacy**

Grade level: **PreK-2**

Percent low income: **75%**

Cost to complete: **$355**

I am a pre-K teacher at a Title I school with a vast majority of students who come from low socio-economic backgrounds. I have 40 students and 40 unique and deserving families who are in need of support. Many of our parents express a desire to help their children's learning through at-home activities; however, they lack the materials and support and thus feel frustrated.

I would love to make take-home literacy backpacks that offer reading materials,

# Appendix

activities, and supplies needed to help support our families and their children's literacy. Kaplan Early Learning Company has the perfect activity kits for these backpacks. The kits give parents real support for building reading skills at home. The literacy sets I have chosen feature six different literacy kits with varied books and activities to reinforce basic skills, which these children will need for success in school and beyond. One of the best things is that each pack comes with all the materials the children need to complete the activities, so no matter what resources children have at home they will be able to successfully complete the activities.

I will send home these literacy packs on a rotating basis so every family has the opportunity to share in this wonderful program. We could really use some strong research-based kits like these to help give our parents the support they need to help their children grow both academically and through parent/child interaction. The cost of the six types of literacy kits including the Comparing Literacy Math Kit is $355, including shipping and fulfillment.

## Children's Books

**Scholastic Book Clubs, Inc.**

Firefly (Preschool)

Honeybee (Toddler-Fours)

See Saw (K-1)

Lucky (Grades 2-3)

Club Leo (Spanish/English PreK-8)
    2931 East McCarty Street
    P.O. Box 7503
    Jefferson City, MO 65102-7503
    800-724-6527
    http://teacher.scholastic.com/clubs/index.htm#firefly

## Checkout System Resources

DEMCO, Inc.
    Self-adhesive book pockets and checkout cards
    P.O. Box 7488
    Madison, WI 53707-7488
    800-962-4463  – Fax: 800-245-1329
    www.demco.com

### Highsmith

Self-adhesive book pockets and checkout cards
800-558-2110
Fax: 800-835-2329
www.highsmith.com

## Suppliers of Take-Home Literacy Packs

**Childcraft Education Corp.**
    Literacy bags, theme bags
    P.O. Box 3239
    Lancaster, PA 17604
    800-631-5652
    Fax: 888-532-4453
    www.childcrafteducation.com

### Innovative Educators

Bookworm Kids Pre-Kindergarten Take-Home Literacy Program
P.O. Box 520
Montezuma, GA 31063
888-252-KIDS
478-472-0164
Fax: 888-536-8553
www.innovative-educators.com

### Lakeshore Learning Materials

Take-home learning packs
2695 E. Dominguez St.
Carson, CA 90895
800-421-5354
Fax: 800-537-5403
http://www.lakeshorelearning.com/

### Pearson Learning Group

Dominie Home Connection Kits (also available in Spanish)
1949 Kellog Avenue

Carlsbad, CA 92008
800-232-4570
Fax: 760-431-8777
http://k12catalog.pearson.com

**Teachers' Bags, Books, and Beyond**
Thematic take-home literacy bags
6050 Shaw Hills Court
Winston Salem, NC 27107
literacy bags: 336-201-8427
Carson-Dellosa resources: 336-476-5988
felt sets: 336-880-5495
Fax: 866- 416-6513
www.teachersbagsbooksandbeyond.com

**Teacher-Created Literacy Bag Resources**

Bee Happy Teaching
http://www.beehappyteaching.com/kinderbuddies.htm

Hubbard's Cupboard
http://www.hubbardscupboard.org/literacy_kits.html

Kinderpond
www.kinderpond.com/discoverypacks.html

Ms. Levin
http://www.pre-kpages.com/buddy_bags.html

Ms. Solley's Traveling Bags
http://www.madison.k12.al.us/mtcarmel/0_kindergarten/solley/bagpage.html

Ponton's Pond
http://myschoolonline.com/page/0,1871,12026-171840-15-46361,00.html

Take-Home Literacy Bags
www.mrsdryzal.com/literacybags.html

Teacher's Corner
http://warhawks.k12.mo.us/elem/klenkew/TeachersKornerBackpacks.html

Traveling Bags
http://www.mrsmcdowell.com/traveling%20bags.htm

**Take-Home Bag Vendors**

**Crystal Springs Books**
Book Buddy Bags
10 Sharon Road, P.O. Box 500
Peterborough, NH 03458
800-321-0401
Fax: 866-604-7367
http://www.crystalspringsbooks.com

**Steps to Literacy**
Pack-N-Read Packs
Buddy Pack Clear Backpack
P.O. Box 6737
Bridgewater, NJ 08807
800-895-2804
Fax: 866-560-8699
www.stepstoliteracy.com

**Book Awards**

**Caldecott Medal**

**American Library Association**
Association for Library Service to Children
50 Huron Street
Chicago, IL 60611
800-545-2433 ext. 2163
Fax: 312-280-5271
http://www.ala.org/ala/alsc/awardsscholarships/literaryawds/caldecottmedal/caldecottmedal.htm

**Children's Book Showcase**
The Children's Book Council
12 West 37th Street, 2nd Floor
New York, NY 10018-7480
212-966-1990
Fax: 212-966-2073
Toll-free fax: 888-807-9355
Orders only: 800-999-2160
http://www.cbcbooks.org/contact.html

**Sources of Book-Related Items**

**American Library Association**
ALA Order Fulfillment
P.O. Box 932501
Atlanta, GA 31193-2501

# Appendix

866-SHOPALA
Fax: 770-280-4155
ala-orders@PBD.com
800-545-2433, press 7
www.alastore.ala.org

**Oriental Trading Post**
P.O. Box 2308
Omaha, NE 68103-2308
800-875-8480
www.orientaltrading.com

**The Library Store**
P.O. Box 964
Tremont, IL 61568
800-548-7204
www.thelibrarystore.com

**Upstart**
W5527 State Road 106
P.O. Box 800
Fort Atkinson, WI 53538-0800
800-448-4887
http://www.highsmith.com

**U.S. Toy**
13201 Arrington Road
Grandview, MO 64030
800-832-0224 – Fax: 816-761-9295
www.ustoy.com

## Sample Library Procedures for Training Teachers and Volunteers

Every program must develop its own procedures. Adapt the ideas in these sample materials to fit the circumstances of any classroom lending library.

### Check-Out Resources

Each program site will have a library of books that are available for children to check out and take home to read with parents. Materials that are needed for this include:

- **Library pockets** glued into the back cover of each book with an **index card** inserted into the pocket listing the title and author of the book.
- A **poster** displayed in the classroom with library pockets mounted on the poster board. Children's names are written on the pockets.
- **Baskets or tubs** containing an assortment of books of various genres, levels, and themes. Books are displayed cover-first for easy selection.
- **Tips for families** explaining why it is important to read with children; ideas on how to share books; sample questions to ask before, during, and/or after reading; how to record their reading on the family reading record sheet; and when to return the book to school.
- Reusable poly-envelopes/heavy-duty sealable bags/backpacks to be used as **take-home book packets** with the child's name, the school's name, address, and phone number.
- **Reading record sheet** for parents to record the title of the book that was read, date, and sign.

### Checkout Procedures

Classroom teacher(s) manage this book checkout process:

- **Children choose the book(s)** that they would like to take home. Discuss the choice and look through the book together (picture walk/predict/discuss vocabulary). If the child wishes, read parts of the book. Children may change their minds. Do not choose the book for the child. If a child is having difficulty, pick out three or four books that you think might be of interest and tell the child why the books might be enjoyable.
- **Remove the card** from the pocket at the back of the book. Write the student's name and date on the card (or ask the child to do so).

- **Place the book card** in the child's pocket on the checkout poster.
- **Place the book** in the take-home bag/backpack along with the family reading record/log and tips for families to share books.

### Check-In Procedures

When children return their books:

- **Engage in a friendly conversation** about the book. (Ask one or two questions such as: What did you enjoy most about this book? What happened first? Next? Last? What was your favorite part? Did the story remind you of something that you or your family do? Was it like another story or book you know?)
- **Remove the book card** from the check-out poster. Check off/draw a line through the child's name showing return of the book. Replace the book card in the back of the book.
- **Check the reading record/log** to see if an adult family member signed and recorded the book. If the log is full, replace with a new one. Place the full log in the child's portfolio.
- **Encourage children to choose another book.**

### Frequently Asked Questions

**How will children know how to take care of books?**

- Model the right way to handle books BEFORE sending them home. Show children how to carefully turn pages, close the book before returning it to the take-home bag, and keep the book dry and in a safe place. Show confidence in children to take care of the books and give them ownership to be responsible for the books.

**How often can a child take a book home? How many?**

- Classroom teachers determine the routine, frequency, and any goals for the number of books children read with their families.

**What do I do if a parent is not reading books with the child?**

- Start by talking with the family to learn about circumstances and attitudes that affect their participation. Together, find ways to overcome any barriers or reluctance. Explain the importance of families taking an active role in their children's learning.
- Invite the family to observe a teacher or parent volunteer read a book with the child. This opportunity might be scheduled, for example, during the time the parents usually drop off or pick up the child so that it is a natural way to invite them to stay for a few moments while the book is finished.
- If the parents are unable to read for whatever reason, together figure out whether a sibling, neighbor, or other volunteer might be interested in participating.
- Offer recordings to listen to in the car or at home.

**What if a child does not return a book?**

- Send the Friendly Reminder note to the family. If the book is lost, record the title and date on the book inventory list so that it can be replaced. If lateness/loss is a recurring problem with a family, set up a time to discuss the importance of returning books so other children can share them, too.

**What if a book is returned damaged?**

- If it is repairable, put the book in the Book Hospital Basket so a volunteer can repair. If not, list it on the book inventory list to be reordered.

Have fun and happy reading!

# Appendix D

## Resources for Involving Families

Many families are eager to help design and implement a classroom lending library. Personal communication with families – to exchange information, share ideas, and plan strategies – are essential to the success of a lending library. These forms can help recruit and maintain families' commitment to an early literacy program. Adapt them to suit the needs of families and the early childhood program.

## Sample Family Survey

> **When Can We Get Together?**
>
> We're planning an informal get-together to share ideas about how to help young children enjoy learning to read. Which of these times is best for your family?
>
> ☐ 8 am ☐ 10 am ☐ 12 noon
> ☐ 2 pm ☐ 4 pm ☐ 6 pm
> ☐ 7 pm ☐ other:
>
> What day(s) do you prefer?
> _____
>
> Child care, door prizes, and refreshments!

## Sample Family Orientation Flyer

> **Family Fun With Books!**
> Presented by the Early Reading First Staff
>
> When: Tuesday, September 30, 7 pm
> Where: Bethel Baptist Church
> 1120 Arlington Ave.
> Child care, door prizes, and refreshments!

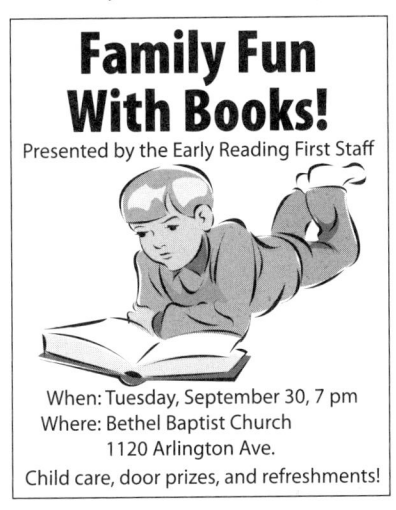

## Sample Family Orientation Agenda

Early Reading First Presents
Family Fun With Books!

- Getting to know each other
- Why read together at home?
- How your lending library works
- Fun follow-up activities
- Questions?
- Refreshments

## Sample Family Orientation Handout

> **How Your Lending Library Works**
>
> - Children bring home books each week to read with their families.
> - An adult shows children how to gently care for books.
> - An adult or older child reads the book with younger children. Grandparents, neighbors, and family friends might also enjoy a turn!
> - An adult fills in the reading log and returns it with the book the next day.
> - Each book includes tips for reading and a few fun follow-up activities.
>
> Try something new – and revisit favorite early reading experiences – each time you share a book!

## Sample Take-Home Tips

Laminate a brief reminder like this to enclose with lending library books when children take them home.

Dear Family,

Reading books aloud together is the best way for families to help children enjoy learning to read. Your child chose this book to read with you! Here are some tips for having fun while you read.

How can we read together?

- With your child, find a quiet, comfortable place to read. Sit close – on your lap is perfect! Hold the book so both of you can see the words and pictures.

## Sharing Books Together:
*Promoting Emergent Literacy Through Reading Aloud and Home-School Partnerships*

- Introduce the book. Look at the cover. Read the title and the names of the author and illustrator. Show your child how to take care of the book by handling it gently.
- Leaf through the book to look at the pictures in the beginning. What does your child notice?
- If you know the story, build excitement! Say how much you enjoy the story. Ask your child to predict what might happen in the book.
- As you read, run your finger or a bookmark (why not make one?) underneath the words. This helps a child realize that you are reading words.
- Be a ham! Use loud and soft voices, squeaky and gruff voices. Make the characters seem almost alive!
- Encourage your child to ask questions. Maybe she or he wonders what a word means. Or why something is happening in the illustrations. Try to figure out the answers together from the rest of the story. You'll learn more about your child with each question asked!
- Notice how the pictures were drawn or painted. Some are photographs. Look for familiar things and items mentioned in the story.
- Invite your child to read repeated words or phrases along with you. Have fun with rhyming words by making up your own verses.
- Link events in the book with similar events in your child's life.
- Ask questions to expand your child's understanding while reading: What do you think could happen next? Why? How would you feel if that happened?
- Use puppets or dolls to act out the story. Do an art project to follow up on the ideas in the book. See the activity guide inside the book for more suggestions.
- At the end of book, ask a few questions, too: What was your favorite part? What happened first? Next? Last? Invite your child to go back and reread or retell the story again. Most books are more fun the more times they are read!

Before you return the book tomorrow, please

- write the title and date on the reading log form
- sign your initials
- tuck the book and form into the book bag

We know you are very busy, so take a break and relax by reading – with your children and curled up with a book for yourself! HAPPY READING!

### Sample Reading Log

| We Enjoyed These Books Together! |||
| --- | --- | --- |
| Child _____ |||
| Teacher _____ |||
| Date | Name of Book | Family Initials |
|  |  |  |
|  |  |  |
|  |  |  |
|  |  |  |
|  |  |  |
|  |  |  |
|  |  |  |
|  |  |  |

### Sample Reminder to Return Books

**We're Missing a Book!**

Dear Family,
Your child checked out: _____
from our class library on: _____
Please return it to school tomorrow so your child can take home another wonderful book – and someone else can enjoy this one!
Thanks so much!
　　　Your teacher, _____

# References

Allington, R. (2000). *What really matters for struggling readers: Designing research based programs.* Boston: Allyn & Bacon.

Anderson, R.C., Hiebert, E.H., Scott, J.A., & Wilkinson, A.G. (1985). *Becoming a nation of readers: The report of the Commission on Reading.* Washington, DC: National Institute of Education.

Appleby, A.N., Langer, J.A., & Mullis, M. (1988). *Who reads best? Factors related to reading achievement in grades 3, 7, and 11.* Princeton, NJ: Educational Testing Service.

Barrentine, S. (1996). *Engaging young children with reading through interactive read-alouds. The Reading Teacher, 50,* 36-43.

batTzedek, E. (2002). *Creating a classroom literacy environment: A guide for childcare, Head Start, and pre-kindergarten teachers.* Philadelphia, PA: Children's Literacy Initiative.

Bear, D., Invernizzi, M., Templeton, S., & Johnston, F. (2000). *Words their way: Word study for phonics, vocabulary, and spelling instruction.* Upper Saddle River, NJ: Merrill Prentice-Hall.

Bennett-Armistad, V.S., Duke, N.K., & Moses, A.M. (2005). *Literacy and the youngest learner: Best practices for educators of children birth to 5.* New York: Scholastic.

Bishop, A.G. (2003). *Prediction of first grade reading achievements: A comparison of fall and winter kindergarten screenings. Learning Disability Quarterly, 26(3),* 189-202.

Blok, H. (1999). *Reading to young children in educational settings: A meta-analysis of recent research. Language Learning, 49(2),* 343-372.

Brock, D., & Dodd, E. (1994). *A family lending library: Promoting early literacy development. Young Children, 49(3),* 16-21.

Brown, J. (1994). *Parent workshops: Closing the gap between parents and teachers. Focus on Early Childhood Education Newsletter, 7(1).*

Bus, A. (2001). *Joint caregiver-child storybook reading: A route to literacy development.* In S. Neuman & D. Dickinson (Eds.), *Handbook of early literacy research* (pp. 179-191). New York: Guilford Press.

Bus, A.G., van Ijzendoorn, M.H., & Pellegrini, A.D.. (1995). *Joint book reading makes for success in learning to read: A meta-analysis on intergenerational transmission of literacy. Review of Education Research, 65(1),* 1-21.

Catts, H.W., Fey, M.E., Zhang, X., & Tomblin, J.B. (1999). *Language basis of reading and reading disabilities: Evidence from a longitudinal investigation. Scientific Studies of Reading, 3,* 331-361.

Chaney, C. (1998). *Preschool language and metalinguistic skills are links to reading success. Applied Psycholinguistics, 19,* 447-462.

Clay, M.M. (2005). *An observation survey of early literacy achievement* (2nd ed.). Auckland, NZ: Heinemann.

Cowley, J. (1983). *Along came greedy cat.* Wellington, NZ: Learning Media.

Cunningham, P. (2000). *Phonics they use* (3rd. ed.). New York: HarperCollins

De Temple, J., & Snow, C. (2003). *Learning words from books.* In A. van Kleeck, S.A. Stahl, & E.B. Bauer (Eds.), *On reading books to children: Parents and teachers* (pp. 16-33). Mahwah, NJ: Erlbaum.

Dickinson, D.K., & Tabors, P.O. (2001). *Beginning literacy with language.* Baltimore: Brookes.

Duncan, P. (1997). *Four famished foxes and Fosdyke.* New York: Harper Trophy.

Durkin, D. (1966). *Children who read early.* New York: Teachers College Press.

Gibbons, G. (1991). *Monarch butterfly.* New York: Holiday House.

Goldenberg, C. (2002). *Making schools work for low-income families in the 21st century.* In S.B. Neuman & D.K. Dickinson (Eds.), *Handbook of early literacy research* (pp. 211-231). New York: Guilford.

Goswami, U. (2001). *Early phonological development and the acquisition of literacy.* In S.B. Neuman & D.K. Dickinson (Eds.), *Handbook of early literacy research* (pp. 111-125). New York: Guilford.

Goswami, U., & Bryant, P. (1990). *Phonological skills and learning to read: Essays in developmental psychology.* London: Psychology Press.

Greaney, V., & Hegarty, M. (1987). *Correlates of leisure-time reading. Journal of Research in Reading, 10(1),* 3-20.

Greene, C. (1997). *Police officers protect people.* Chanhassan, MN: Child's World.

Greenfield, E. (2004). *In the land of words: New and selected poems.* New York: HarperCollins.

Hart, B., & Risley, T.R. (1995). *Meaningful differences in the everyday experience of young American children.* Baltimore: Brookes.

Heath, S.B. (1983). *Ways with words: Language, life, and work in communities and classrooms.* New York: Cambridge University Press.

Jalongo, M.R. (2004). *Young children and picture books* (2nd ed.). Washington, DC: National Association for the Education of Young Children.

Jansky, J., & de Hirsch, K. (1972). *Preventing reading failure – Prediction, diagnosis, intervention.* New York: Harper & Row.

Justice, L.M., & Ezell, H.K. (2000). *Enhancing children's print and word awareness through home-based parent intervention. American Journal of Speech-Language Pathology, 9(3),* 257-269.

Justice, L.M., & Ezell, H.K. (2002). *Use of storybook reading to increase print awareness in at-risk children. American Journal of Speech-Language Pathology, 11(1),* 17-29.

Kamii, C., & Manning, M. (1999). *Before "invented" spelling: Kindergartners' awareness that writing is related to the sounds of speech. Journal of Research in Childhood Education, 14(1),* 16-25.

Krashen, S. (1993). *Power of reading: Insights from the research.* Englewood, CO: Libraries Unlimited.

Leslie, L., & Caldwell, J. (2005). *Qualitative reading inventory* (4th ed.). Upper Saddle River, NJ: Allyn Bacon Longman.

Levy, A.L., Gong, Z., Hessels, S., Evans, M.A., & Jared, D. (2005). *Understanding print: Early reading development and the contributions of home literacy experiences. Journal of Experimental Child Psychology, 98(1),* 63-93.

Lucerno, J. (1966). *How to make salsa.* New York: Mondo.

Mass, Y., & Cohen, K.A. (2006). *Home connections to learning: Supporting parents as teachers. Young Children, 61(1),* 54-55.

# References

McDonald Connor, C., Son, S., Hindman, A.H., & Morrison, F.J. (2005). *Teacher qualifications, classroom practices, family characteristics, and preschool experience: Complex effects on first graders' vocabulary and early reading outcomes. Journal of School Psychology, 43(4),* 343-375.

Morrow, L.M. (1983). *Home and school correlates of early interest in literature. Journal of Educational Reseach, 75,* 339-344.

Morrow, L.M. (2001). *Literacy development in the early years: Helping children read and write* (4th ed.). Boston: Allyn & Bacon.

Morrow, L.M., & Weinstein, C. (1986). *Encouraging voluntary reading: The importance of a literature program on children's use of library centers. Reading Research Quarterly, 21,* 330-346.

Morrow, L.M., & Young, J. (1997). *A family literacy program connecting school and home: Effects on attitude, motivation, and literacy achievement. Journal of Educational Psychology, 89(4),* 736-743.

Muter, V., Hulme, C., & Snowling, M.J. (2004). *Phonemes, rimes, vocabulary, and grammatical skills as foundations of early reading development: Evidence from a longitudinal study. Developmental Psychology, 40(5),* 665-681.

Neuman, S.B., Celano, D.C., Greco, A.N., & Shue, P. (2001). *Access for all: Closing the book gap for children in early education.* Newark, DE: International Reading Association.

Neuman, S.B., & Dickinson, D.K. (Eds.). (2001). *Handbook of early literacy research.* New York: Guilford.

Numeroff, L. (1991). *If you give a moose a muffin.* New York: Laura Geringer/Harper Collins.

Prescott, O. (1965). *A father reads to his children.* New York: Dutton.

Rathman, P. (1995). *Officer Buckle and Gloria.* New York: Putnam.

Reese, E., Cox, A., Harte, D., & McAnally, H. (2003). *Diversity in adults' styles of reading books to children.* In A. van Kleeck, S.A. Stahl, & E.B. Bauer (Eds.), *On reading books to children: Parents and teachers* (pp. 16-33). Mahwah, NJ: Erlbaum.

Ritchey, K.D., & Speece, D.L. (2006). *From letter naming to word reading: The nascent role of sublexical fluency. Contemporary Educational Psychology, 31(3),* 301-327.

Rupley, W. (2005). *Vocabulary knowledge: Its contribution to reading growth and development.* Reading & Writing Quarterly, 21, 203–20.

Sayeski, K.L., Burgess, K.A., Pianta, R.C., & Lloyd, J.W. (2001). *Literacy behaviors of preschool children participating in an early intervention program* (CIERA Rep. No. 2-014). Ann Arbor: University of Michigan, Center for the Improvement of Early Reading Achievement.

Scanlon, D.M., & Vellutino, F.R. (1996). *Prerequisite skills, early instruction, and success in first grade reading: Selected results from a longitudinal study. Mental Retardation and Developmental Research Reviews, 2,* 54-63.

Scarborough, H.S. (1998). *Early identification of children at risk for reading disabilities: Phonological awareness and some other promising predictors.* In B.K. Shapiro, A.J. Capute, & B. Shapiro (Eds.). *Specific reading disability: A view of the spectrum.* Hillsdale, NJ: Erlbaum.

Scarborough, H.S. (2001). *Connecting early language and literacy to later* reading (dis)abilities: Evidence, theory and practice. In S.B. Neuman & D.K. Dickinson (Eds.), *Handbook of early literacy research* (pp. 97-110). New York: Guilford.

Snow, C., Burns, M., & Griffin, P. (1998). *Preventing reading difficulties in young children.* Washington, DC: National Academy Press.

Sonnenschein, S., & Munsterman, K. (2002). *The influence of home-based reading interactions on 5-year-olds' reading motivations and early literacy development. Early Childhood Research Quarterly, 17,* 318-337.

Storch, S.S., & Whitehurst, G.J. (2002). *Oral language and code-related precursors to reading: Evidence from a longitudinal structural model. Developmental Psychology, 38,* 934-947.

Sulzby, E., & Edwards, P. (1993). *The role of parents in supporting literacy development of young children.* In B. Spodek & O. Saracho (Eds.), *Language and literacy in early childhood education: Vol. 4, Yearbook in early childhood education,* pp. 156-177. New York: Teachers College Press.

Talan, C. (1990, November). *Family literacy: Libraries doing what libraries do best.* Wilson Library Bulletin, 65(3), 30-32, 158.

Taylor, D., & Dorsey-Gaines, C. (1988). *Growing up literate: Learning from inner-city families.* Portsmouth, NH: Heinemann.

Trelease, J. (2001). *The read-aloud handbook* (5th ed.). New York: Penguin.

Vukelich, C., Christie, J., & Enz, B. (2002). *Helping young children learn language and literacy.* Boston: Allyn & Bacon.

Whitehurst, G.J., & Lonigan, C.J. (2001). *Emergent literacy: Development from pre-readers to readers.* In S.B. Neuman & D.K. Dickinson (Eds.), *Handbook of early literacy research* (pp. 11-29). New York: Guilford.

Yopp, H. (1995). *Read-aloud books for developing phonemic awareness: An annotated bibliography. Reading Teacher, 48,* 538-541.